Prai
Heartset® Education

"Stu Semigran's commitment and love for young people fills each page. He sees the beauty of what their lives can become and he shares ways they can get there by building their resilience. He is a master teacher of the heart!"
— Arianna Huffington, Founder & CEO, Thrive Global

Stu brings simple wisdom and practical tools for empowering young people everywhere. He draws upon the vast wealth of his experience with schools, educators and students worldwide in this wonderful and timely new book."
— Pedro A. Noguera, PhD, Dean, Rossier School of Education, Distinguished Professor of Education, University of Southern California

"Heartset® Education teaches valuable life skills that all children need to create successful, fulfilling and meaningful lives. I highly recommend this book."
— Jack Canfield, Co-creator of the *Chicken Soup for the Soul®* series and Author of *The Success Principles*™: *How to Get from Where You Are to Where You Want to Be*

"Stu's book Lights up the new way of education. At last we embrace the greatest truth: Loving is the way into the hearts of our children, exciting them to learn, healing their pain with trust, and showing them how to build a strong core of Heartset resiliency."
— Leigh Taylor-Young, Emmy Award-winning Actress, Ordained Minister, and prior Goodwill Environmental Ambassador for the UN

"If you care about the future of our world, based on the young people growing up in it, this book is a must-read. It should be a required manual for anyone dealing with kids (and, frankly, dealing with yourself). I challenge anyone reading this not to be moved about something important, inside. Bravo, Stu!"
— David Allen, Author of Getting Things Done: The Art of Stress-Free Productivity

"Lighthearted and deeply transformative, *Heartset Education* sets the groundwork for our educational system shifting to a kind and thoughtful understanding of the greater needs of our children."
— Parker J. Palmer, author of *On the Brink of Everything*, *A Hidden Wholeness*, and *The Courage to Teach*

"*Heartset Education* brings to light the need for educating every child with greater love and understanding. It should be at the core for all our schools!"
— Michael Funk, Director, Expanded Learning Division for the California Department of Education

"If you're a parent, you need to read this book. If you're a teacher, you really need to read this book. If you're a student, you're praying that your parents and teachers read this book. Stu's powerful and insightful book encourages us to educate and respect the whole person—body, mind and heart."
— Russell Bishop, author of *From Self-Talk to Soul-Talk: Becoming More of Who You Truly Are*

"*Heartset Education: A Way of Living and Learning* is a terrific book and needs to be read by all educators. I've been involved with Stu and EduCare over the previous 30 years and had an opportunity to interact with some of his students, parents and staff. What Stu writes about is lived by his staff and of course himself. In short, the results are amazing. You can see it in the smiles and shining eyes of students in EduCare's programs. Educating young people to adopt that belief in themselves will provide a head start wherever EduCare's students decide to contribute to the world."

— Gregory Stebbins, Ed.D., Founder and
Master Coach, PeopleSavvy

Heartset Education explores the power of teaching to the heart and soul of our young people. Thankful for you, Stu, and for your many years of loving kids into life giving change!"

— Bill Milliken, Founder and Vice-Chairman of
Communities In Schools, Inc.

"At last. We've waited too long for this book and to address what is most needed in teaching our young people—opening their hearts as well as educating their minds! We can't recommend it strongly enough."

— Ron and Mary Hulnick, Founding Faculty and
Co-Directors of the University of Santa Monica

"Child and youth development research continues to highlight that when children, youth, and their families experience love it is healing, and supports positive developmental outcomes. In this text, Stu Semigran beautifully illustrates WHY love is the foundation of education and youth development work. Perhaps more importantly, Stu demonstrates HOW the environments and experiences we create for children and their families can be rooted in this foundation of love, resulting in powerful and transformative outcomes."

— Jeff Davis, Executive Director,
California AfterSchool Network (CAN)

"In this brilliantly written book, Stu lays the foundation of education In the Centre of the HEART and reminds us of the wise paradigm of Heartset to guide the educators to use the skills and the tools to educate with the emphasis to awaken the heart of each student. Learning then becomes filled with enthusiasm, joy and upliftment. It is a guide that will help everyone remember that when we live from the heart, we live in fullness of who we are, tapping into our potential, and serving our fellow human beings."

— Agapi Stassinopoulos, Author of *Speaking with Spirit: 52 Prayers to Guide, Inspire and Uplift You*

"Stu Semigran's delightful storytelling reveals how love can heal our children's pain and build an inner personal core of resiliency."

— Keith Leon S., 7x Award-Winning 9x International
Bestselling Author, Speaker, and Publisher

"Stu's *Heartset Education* is filled with inspiring stories, a new mindset, and practical methods for touching young people's hearts and preparing them for future leadership roles. I recommend this book for any teacher, parent, or leader that wants to make a meaningful and positive impact on the lives of others."

— Mark Samuel, founder and CEO of IMPAQ and
author of *B State*

"*Heartset Education* is a MUST for bringing the best out of both educators and parents!"
— Gloria Halley, Region 2 Lead for Learning Support, Expanded Learning Service, Office of Education, Butte County (CA)

"Stu sparks the awareness that establishing a foundation of love in our families, our classrooms, and our society, is essential for the well-being of all of our children."
— Sam Piha, Founder, Temescal Associates and The How Kids Learn Foundation

"I wholeheartedly recommend Stu Semigran's *Heartset Education!* I have had the distinct pleasure of watching Stu work his Heartset magic in person with remarkable results, and now all can benefit from his decades of leadership in the field of Social Emotional Learning (SEL) by reading his book. This book offers effective methods for touching our young people's hearts, opening their minds, and changing their lives."
— Dr. Amy Cranston, Executive Director, SEL4CA

"Stu Semigran's *Heartset Education* is a revelation. Having known Stu since I was in school myself, I know his dedication to assisting young people in recognizing their intrinsic value. Imagine our world if our schools taught our children from a place of love."
— Joe Hubbard, Chief Training Officer at Thrive Global

Heartset® Education

Heartset® Education

A Way of Living and Learning

Stu Semigran
President and Co-Founder, EduCare Foundation

Copyright © 2022 Stu Semigran

Published by EduCare Foundation
Paperback ISBN: 978-1-7359130-3-2
Ebook ISBN: 978-1-7359130-4-9

*To all children across the world and
all those who love, serve, and lift them*

Contents

Introduction

How many of us see potential in our kids that they don't see?

We can see their lives stretching out in front of them. They don't see it. How do we wake kids up to who they are and what their lives could become?

It isn't a mystery. There are ways to build a sense of connection, relationship, compassion, forgiveness, and understanding in a classroom. It can't be done entirely with curriculum or subject matter content. It's also in the environment, the culture, and the community that surrounds our kids. It is in the people.

Students need to have their minds ready to learn. However, to become active learners, a lot of our kids need more than that. They don't just need a new mindset; they need a new *heartset*. When the heart is set in a good place, the mind is open and receptive. When heart is troubled, the mind is cluttered. So heart and mind have to go hand in hand.

I am suggesting a new way to look at education that I call *Heartset® Education*. Most people are familiar with the idea of a good mindset, a frame of mind that is positive and affirming. *Heartset* is a *frame of heart*. It is the power of unconditional love, where love is the foundation for education.

Heartset Education lays the nurturing soil from which the seeds of vibrant teaching, parenting, and learning sprout. Kindness of heart establishes an energy of self-awareness, non-judgment (acceptance), peace, caring, positivity, giving, forgiveness, and compassion. *Heartset* creates an empathetic environment in

15

which our young people—and the rest of us—can flourish in spite of the uncertainties and challenges we all face.

Somehow, I intuitively knew this concept when I was just starting out as a young teacher. Working at an underserved middle school in Los Angeles in 1978, I could see that what was being attempted in public education was missing the mark for our kids. So many young people seemed to be lost, awkwardly trying to maneuver through the troubles and traumas of their lives.

I wondered: *What if we could teach them greater self-awareness, as well as coping, social, and practical life skills? We could make their lives easier and their futures brighter. We could help them treat themselves and each other with greater kindness and understanding.*

I asked my middle school principal if I could start teaching a class in self-awareness, social skills, and character development. I didn't have a good name for it at the time. His reply was a clear *no* followed by, "You need to get those test scores up."

Not taking *no* for an answer, I found a way to discreetly work around the issue. I started teaching elements of these essential life skills to the students in my classes. The class atmosphere soon came alive. Smiles, laughter, and friendships sparked, enriched by deep and honest discussion. As this learning environment of kindness, empathy, and caring was built, test scores significantly rose. Soon after, when the principal heard word of the results, it became an established elective class.

This became the impetus for me to extend the curriculum even further. In 1990, with my wife and fellow teacher, Candace, I launched *EduCare*. Our heartfelt intention for EduCare was to touch the lives of more students by establishing love as a foundation in their education. As a non-profit organization, our mission became *to inspire and empower young people to become responsible citizens and compassionate leaders and to live their dreams.*

EduCare Foundation now supports over 30,000 students annually across more than 100 elementary, middle, and high schools in Southern California with social-emotional learning (SEL) programs, afterschool programs, and case management. Since 1990, over 300,000 students have benefitted from EduCare's direct student services. Over 45,000 teachers and parents across more than 500 schools have participated in EduCare professional development programs and parent workshops throughout the United States and abroad.

Bringing love front and center in education in ways that are understandable, practical, field-tested, and evaluated has been at the core of *Heartset Education*. Education is moving away from gauging success primarily by test scores. We are moving toward an understanding of the need for whole-child education that is heart-centered and includes social-emotional learning. We must educate the intellect, the heart, and the character of our young people with a clear focus on equity and inclusion.

More and more educational leaders are understanding the truth in this saying (author unknown, but commonly attributed to Aristotle):

> *Educating the mind without educating the heart*
> *is no education at all.*

This ideal is captured in a statement from a high school principal after his students and teachers participated in EduCare's ACE (Achievement and Commitment to Excellence) Student Success Program: "EduCare, you are teaching from the inside out. You've opened my students' hearts, and now we can capture their minds." He recognized that when the heart is set in a healthy and compassionate place, the mind is more open, available, and prepared to learn.

With this book, I invite you into *Heartset Education: A Way of Living and Learning*, a program based on the eight *Heartset* skills. It is an opportunity for you to look deeply at yourself and at our young people today. Look into their dreams and, with hope in your heart, see what could lie ahead.

The book highlights stories of my students, colleagues, friends, and family members who inspired and advanced the growth of *Heartset*. Each chapter also includes a few engaging *Heartset* activities for teachers, parents, and students, many of them from *Making the Best of Me: a Handbook for Student Excellence and Self-Esteem*.[1]

My sincere wish is that reading *Heartset Education* inspires you to love yourself more deeply. Together, we can learn to strengthen our human connection so that we create families, schools, and communities of greater understanding, empathy, and compassion for our young people.

A portion of the proceeds from the purchase of this book will be donated to the EduCare Foundation to support Heartset educational programs empowering thousands of young people to become courageous and compassionate leaders. To learn more, visit educarefoundation.com

Heartset®
...is a kindness of heart.

It establishes a culture of
self-awareness, empathy,
personal responsibility,
and compassion – to build
genuine communities of caring.

EduCare's Eight *Heartset* Skills

Skill #1   Seeing the Best in Everyone—*Honoring*

Skill #2   Positively Reinforcing—*Praising*

Skill #3   Listening From the Heart

Skill #4   The Power of Choice—*Personal Responsibility*

Skill #5   Resolving Conflict

Skill #6   Moving From Judgment to Forgiveness

Skill #7   Turning Challenges Into Learning Opportunities

Skill #8   Giving and Receiving

Chapter One

Seeing the Best in Everyone— *Honoring*

The question is not what you look at, but what you see.
— Henry David Thoreau

Seeing the best in everyone is seeing the best in ourselves, our students, our family, friends, coworkers, and even strangers. When we honor each person—their uniqueness, specialness, gifts, and talents—we demonstrate to them our unconditional positive regard and respect.

Honoring is defined as "respecting, admiring, revering, venerating, or paying tribute to."[2] We generally understand that we should honor others, but do we honor ourselves? Honoring is founded in the compassion we have for ourselves and in learning to see the best in ourselves.

Why do we have a hard time seeing the best in ourselves? Do we think we have to prove our self-worth by how much we do or accomplish? Perhaps we've been taught, sought out, and subsequently gained approval when we've done something right or succeeded in someone else's eyes. Then, we directed ourselves by saying: *The more I do, the better I am. If I do more, prove myself to others, and gain their approval, then I'll feel that I'm okay.*

That approval-seeking, or looking to being honored by other people, is a bumpy road. Seeking approval from others is like trying to fill an endless void. It is so tenuous, so dependent on others' opinions—what they value, what they think. It's ever-so fragile because those *approval gains* shift moment to moment. Then what happens to our self-worth?

Being Enough

I grew up in a Jewish family in Brooklyn, New York. We moved *up* to Queens and then, as my father prospered more, out to Long Island. I was a good son—working hard, trying to show off my abilities, trying to gain praise from those around me.

When I returned home from school one day in fourth or fifth grade, I was excited to show my dad and mom how well I did on a test. I proudly showed my dad the score. It was 93 percent.

I can still hear my dad asking, "What happened to those other seven points?"

Not only did I then think the test score wasn't good enough, I internalized that maybe the score was about me—maybe *I just wasn't good enough.* So, my quiet decision-maker mobilized to prove my value to others. *I will show them and prove I'm enough.*

What did I truly desire? To know for myself that I was enough.

It was a tough treadmill. The *do-do-do* mindset kept me motivated. But at what price? That finish line of *I am enough* was always pushed further and further from me. At first, it was the 93 percent on the test, but then the finish line moved to 95 or 100 percent. Perhaps even a perfect score wouldn't be enough. Later in my life, the finish line was determined by how many college degrees, what type of car, and what type of house I acquired. The finish line of *I am enough* was not getting closer at all. It was tirelessly, continually, moving further away.

After years of striving to cross the finish line of enoughness and to land in a place where I was okay with myself, I despaired. There's a saying: *When you get sick and tired of being tired and sick, you change.* I had reached that point. In my quest to step off the achievement treadmill, I took classes, attended seminars, read self-help books, and deepened my spiritual growth. While attending a class on spiritual psychology, I was reflecting and discussing my life pattern with a friend and had an amazing inner experience. I saw a Higher Being handing back my exam paper. On the top was written: Pass. It wasn't a 93. It wasn't a 100—just the word Pass.

I broke out laughing, realizing the importance of this image. I understood that, when I came into this world, I already had *passed*. I didn't need to do more, prove more, or accomplish more. What I really needed to do was to live, learn, and enjoy my life. Living was not about accomplishing, but rather growing, expressing, and appreciating myself and each moment more fully.

This *aha* instant shook my core, opened my eyes, and flipped my mindset. I got a glimpse of what it would be like to honor myself as I was. I tasted at that moment what it was to deeply accept myself the way I am; it was as if a burden had been lifted. A gentler, more inner directive began to take root.

Then the next and bigger questions became: How do I switch from basing my self-approval on my actions and how others perceive them to what I'd easily and generously approve for myself? Would I continue to win my self-approval points based on how much I accomplished each day? What if I could move to living in the field of unconditional self-loving, based not on what I did, but simply for who I am? It was time to consciously place value on my *beingness* rather than my *doingness*.

> Do I belong to myself or to others? Is the primary purpose of myself the pursuit of my own happiness and the fulfillment of my own positive potentialities or is it a compliance with the wants and expectations of others? Do I live by my own vision of things or by the vision of others?
>
> — Dr. Nathaniel Brandon, *Honoring the Self: Self-Esteem and Personal Transformation*

What if I could move to living in the field of unconditional self-loving, based not on what I did, but simply for who I am?

Honoring must always start by honoring ourselves. That is a pretty radical thought. Typically, if you honor yourself, you're labeled *conceited*. We and our students need to understand that self-honoring doesn't mean we're above the crowd. It means we're striving to be the best version of ourselves and want to support others to thrive as well.

Jerry

I was teaching in Los Angeles Unified School District at a tough inner-city middle school in one of the poorest neighborhoods of South Los Angeles. I was a rookie teacher, in my early twenties, there to do whatever I could do to wake up kids to who they were and what their lives could become. One of my students was Jerry, a bright, likable eighth grader with a delightfully impish sense of humor. Academically, he was slightly below average, though he seemed to be a student who could easily achieve excellent grades.

On the morning of a test day, Jerry meandered into class and stopped by my desk as he often did to say hello. He looked up, smiled a bit, and declared, "You know what? I am going to fail that test today."

I paused a second, looked directly at him, and commented, "Yeah, I bet you are."

He was startled. *What type of remark is that from my history teacher, who is typically a really caring guy?*

"Jerry, if you've already been telling yourself that you'll fail, that's what you'll probably do."

Somewhere along the line, Jerry had learned to give up, to not respect or honor himself. He had little aspiration for where he was going and what his life could become. He appeared— like many other students—headed to give up on himself, his education, his future, and his life. For Jerry, the streets, drugs, and gangs were likely choices.

Self-Acknowledgment Versus Conceit

Self-honoring isn't about being conceited or being a braggart. Differentiating between self-acknowledgment and being conceited is essential. Self-acknowledgment is not built upon being better than another or putting someone down to build up the self. Consider the difference in these two statements:

- I'm an excellent teacher.
- I'm the best teacher in this school.

The first statement is self-acknowledgment; the second statement puts others below oneself.

Our students often balk at the idea of acknowledging or seeing the best of themselves. They are wary of being seen as conceited and often confuse positive self-image with superiority or vanity. Many do not want to appear too smart or too talented, so they diminish their self-regard to fit in. Discussions based on two statements like the examples above often lead students to express their fear of disapproval and, at the same time, to explore how they might base their own self-worth on the opinions of others.

To believe in a dream of building a joyful and rewarding life that is personally fulfilling and contributes to others, a student needs to believe deeply from within that they are worthy and capable of such a dream. If they do not believe in their intrinsic goodness and essential value, then the best of courses with the most advanced educational materials and amazing teachers will fall short.

Self-Compassion

The research-based field of self-honoring and self-compassion has gained a lot of attention.

> Most of us feel compassion when a close friend is struggling. What would it be like to receive the same caring attention whenever you needed it most? All that's required is a shift in the direction of our attention—recognizing that as a human being, you, too, are a worthy recipient of compassion.
> — Dr. Kristin Nieff, Center for Mindful Self-Compassion

Self-compassion involves responding to difficult internal thoughts and feelings with kindness, sympathy, and understanding, so we soothe and comfort ourselves when we're hurting. Research has shown that self-compassion greatly enhances emotional well-being. It boosts happiness, reduces anxiety and depression, and can even help maintain healthy lifestyle habits, such as diet and exercise.

Self-honoring is the foundation. Until we first see the best in ourselves, we aren't able to see the best in others. Honoring ourselves doesn't mean we ignore that we all have qualities to develop and improve. Seeing our less-than-perfect attributes simply doesn't have to get in the way of also seeing the best of who each of us is.

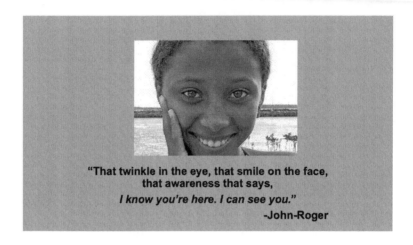

"That twinkle in the eye, that smile on the face, that awareness that says,
I know you're here. I can see you."
-John-Roger

Self-Talk

Of all the people you talk to in your life, the person you talk to the most is yourself. Each day you hatch thousands of thoughts and ideas about who you are and what you are doing. Many of them are repetitive, and the majority are often negative. The way you think and talk about yourself strongly influences your life. We can do something about that.

We also hear hundreds of negative comments daily. Research has shown that an average three-year-old will have twice as many negative comments—*shut up, no, that's bad*—directed their way than positive comments, such as *thanks, good going, great job.*[3] After years of growing up hearing negative comments, children develop the belief that they are who people say they are.

We take to heart and accept others' assessments that we are too tall, too short, too shy, too talkative, too rude, too loud, or too dumb. We are just *not good enough* the way we are. Inside our conversations with ourselves, our self-talk, we create a complicated assortment of doubts and judgments about ourselves. We build the mental habit of being unduly critical about our past and fearful about our future.

What if you are not responsible for every thought you now have, but only the ones you hold in your mind and keep thinking and focusing on? Of all the many habits you may choose to adopt, two of the most harmful are negative self-talk and negative focus.

Positive Focus

For many people, negative self-talk is an addiction. Building the habit of positive self-talk takes awareness and practice.

During my teaching days in Los Angeles, I worked with about 135 middle school students daily. At the end of the school day, I would often think back and obsess about the interactions with three or four students I thought I had messed up on. I may have ignored the students, been impatient with them, or perhaps acted too critically toward them. I forgot to focus, however, on the other 132, whom I had connected with and treated so well.

Researchers continue to cite, apart from life enjoyment, the effects positive self-talk and self-honoring have on health.

> What if you are not responsible for every thought you now have, but only the ones you hold in your mind and keep thinking and focusing on?

The Mayo Clinic cites some health benefits of positive thinking, which include:

- Lower rates of depression
- Lower levels of distress
- Better psychological and physical well-being
- Better coping skills during hardships and times of stress
- Increased life span[4]

Summary

Self-honoring and positive self-talk are perhaps two of the most beneficial gifts a parent, caregiver, or teacher can give their children. Show your caring for your students by honoring yourself. It's been said: *Take care of yourself so that you can then help take care of others.* Being the martyr, the one who is so stressed because they *try so hard* does not work. It does not work for your students, and it certainly does not work for you. By physically, emotionally, mentally, and spiritually honoring yourself, you are, in fact, providing a great example—a positive role model to your students. And when you do, you spontaneously have more within you to give.

In a letter to the *Los Angeles Times* after the tragic school shooting at Saugus High School in 2019, I expressed the essential need for our young people to be seen:

> *Let's imagine schools where human connection and kindness are the norm—where no student would go unnoticed; where students who may want to remain invisible are seen, not forgotten, and are valued and loved; and where both the bullied and bully are noticed and helped.*

Let's look with eyes willing to see each other, not for the differences that we think divide us, but for the goodness of who we each truly are.

Exercises For Educators/Parents

Journal

While working through this book, we recommend you keep a journal for jotting down important thoughts and points as you read them. We also will be sharing journaling exercises for you and your children or students.

1. *My Good News*

   For the next week, at least once daily, reflect on the following: In this moment, what can I acknowledge myself for? *What's the good news about me?*

   Consider capturing three to five examples of good news about you in your journal. Focus more on your inner good news or successes versus stuff you got done. Acknowledge your positive qualities. For instance, rather than writing *I acknowledge myself for cleaning the garage, exercising, and getting a lot done at work,* you might write *I acknowledge myself for my perseverance, my focus, and my strength of purpose.*

2. *One Step Further*

   If you have encountered a challenging situation with another person, look for the goodness in the person. Ask yourself: *Looking past their actions in this moment, what are the positive qualities or attributes I see in this person?*

Self-Talk

1. Is what you're telling yourself worth listening to? Why is it easier at times to be negative about yourself than positive?

2. List at least five negative self-talk statements you often tell yourself. For example:

   No matter what I do, it is never good enough.

   Nothing is going to go right for me today.

   They don't like me.

   No one cares really cares about me.

3. Then list at least ten positive self-talk statements you can say about who you are and what you do. For example:

   I am a great friend who people trust and like.

   I am good at making decisions. I like challenges, and I meet them head on.

   I really am very special. I like who I am, and I feel good about myself.

4. Brag About Yourself—to Yourself

   Take three minutes each day to brag about yourself to yourself. Review all the great things you did today. Speak out loud in front of a mirror, write a list in your journal, or sit back silently with your eyes closed. Choose whichever way you prefer. These can be little things—like helping a family member or friend, complimenting someone, or accomplishing something challenging. You can brag about some of the good things you have done for yourself—like eating healthy foods and taking care of yourself. You can brag about some of the things you are grateful for, something you finally accomplished, having wonderful friendships, or getting along better with your family, friends, or colleagues.

Exercises For Students/Children

Self-Talk Detective

Assign students this homework: *Watch for your negative self-talk and put-downs.* Have everyone scout for these negative statements, and when they are spotted, experiment with switching them to affirming statements.

For example: *Nothing is going right for me today* can pivot to *I am doing my best to handle a really tough day.* As you start to become aware of your own negative self-talk, you may also become more aware of hearing you or others verbalize their negative self-talk.

Self-Acknowledgment

Ask students to make a list of three to five things they would like someone to acknowledge about themselves. These might include:

- *I am a caring friend.*

- *I am a good athlete.*

- *I am good at making decisions.*

Have them either say these out loud in a safe setting, share with a partner, or write in a journal.

Letter to Yourself

Ask your students to write a letter of caring support and encouragement to themselves. Tell them to imagine writing it with as much warmth as if they were writing it to the person they care about the most in the entire world.

In their letters, they should give themselves appreciation, wise advice, acknowledgment for the things they have done well, and forgiveness for the things they are still working on. Ask them to put their caring and understanding for themselves into these private letters. Suggest that they read the letters often, particularly when having a tough day.

Chapter Two

Positively Reinforcing—*Praising*

Praise, like sunlight, helps all things to grow.
— Croft M. Pentz

As a rule, we care. We want the most for our children, our students. As teachers, we may sometimes discover moments when everything seems to be going right. Perhaps we don't really know how or why these positive moments occur. These are the moments when we see a class, a student, or a teacher clearly demonstrating high self-esteem or self-honoring. The learning experience sparkles with aliveness and vitality. The reservoir of self-esteem becomes deeper and, in turn, serves as a solid foundation for future teachable moments.

It is not enough to catch only a few of those shining moments. Our young people are too important. The reasons we devote ourselves to teaching and parenting are too valuable and sincere. We personally deserve to have the satisfaction of making a difference in other lives and experiencing our success.

Self-honoring and praise go hand in hand. There have been times in life when people see the best in us when we don't even see it ourselves. How fortunate that they can see the promise, the gift of who we are, when we are wrapped up in our own harsh self-judgment or turmoil. Their encouragement and reassuring praise may be just the force needed to cut through the barrage of negative messages we may be telling ourselves.

Israel

Around 2000, EduCare was invited to work with Arab and Jewish schools in Israel. On my first day, the teacher came over to me right away, discreetly pointed to a kid, and said, "Be careful. This kid is going to be your trouble in your program."

I thought: *Why is he sharing this with me?* I knew he was trying to help me out, but another part of me thought: *Why is that label already on that kid? I don't even know this boy.*

I asked, "Is there anything about him, this student, that's really outstanding?"

The teacher said, "He's a great artist. He's really good with cartoons and drawing."

> Encouragement and reassuring praise may be just the force needed to cut through the barrage of negative messages we may be telling ourselves.

I realized I had found my way in. Over the next few days, guess who was the banner and poster maker for the program? That student. Who was no trouble in the program? That student.

I chose to not make it a matter of how he might deter the program or me, but rather a matter of how could I see the best in him, take who he was, and bring it forward. Before I left that community, I had a chance to chat with the teacher.

I suggested that this student could soar if mentored by a local artist who could help feed his passion and love for art.

If we can redirect our kids and catch them at their best, then we bring them to where we see them. If we don't let them focus on the negative, we shouldn't have to focus there either.

Impactful Praise

How do we approach praising people so that it is authentic and impactful?

Carol Dweck, social psychologist and esteemed researcher at Stanford University, has been a leading influence in promoting growth mindset and identifying effective methods of praising young people.

In her article "The Perils and Promises of Praise" in *Educational Leadership*, she points out that generic praise given indiscriminately can actually be detrimental. She highlights how "the wrong kind of praise creates self-defeating behavior. The right kind motivates students to learn."[5]

What kind of praise is the right kind? How can we make praise in the classroom effective? A lot of it has to do with the timing, as well as the quality and kind of praise.

Dr. Dweck underscores that praising *intelligence* makes students avoid challenge. As they may face difficulties, they tend to lose any pleasure in a task they had originally enjoyed. As a result, they doubt themselves and their performance drops. In an article in the Stanford University Bing Times, Dweck notes, " . . . intelligence praise puts them in the fixed mindset where what they cared most about was looking smart, and where they couldn't cope with challenges."[6]

Examples of praising intelligence, or inherent ability:

- *You are so smart.*

- *You have a natural talent for drawing.*

- *You have a perfect body for gymnastics.*

Many believe these types of statements increase a student's motivation to achieve and succeed, but this is not the case. Jenny Anderson, senior reporter and editor of *How to be Human*, writes that research shows "that kids who are praised for being smart fixate on performance, shying away from taking risks and meeting potential failure. Kids who are praised for their efforts try harder and persist with tasks longer. These effort kids have a growth mindset marked by resilience and a thirst for mastery; the smart ones have a fixed mindset, believing intelligence to be innate and not malleable."[7]

What if the most effective use of praise is when it's given for effort, hard work, and persistence—known as *praising process* rather than *praising achievement*? Praising their hard work and their grit leads to students wanting to learn for the excitement and adventure of being challenged in their learning. Praising achievement, on the other hand, trains students to seek out other people's approval based on externally placed bars of achievement.

Praising for achievement was a trap I fell into many years ago. Even 95 percent on tests was never good enough. Our young people flourish around adults with growth mindsets who rather than directing them to try to top some externally placed bar of achievement, welcome their mistakes, encourage their determination, and excite their learning process.

Praise also works best when it is tied to specific behaviors. Collette Bennett comments in "Effective Praise in the Classroom:"

> Teachers may give general praise using phrases such as, "Great work!" or "Nice job, students!" General phrases are not the most effective way for teachers to give feedback in the classroom. General phrases are directed to no one or to no skill in particular. Moreover, while these general phrases may be nice to hear, they may be too broad, and their overuse may result in becoming humdrum. Similarly, routine responses such as "Awesome!" or "Excellent!" by themselves do not inform the student what specific behaviors brought about success.[8]

The language of encouragement tied to hard work and specific behavior is essential.

For example:

- I see you really worked hard to complete this project.

The language of encourage-ment tied to hard work and specific behavior is essential.

- I know you might have felt like quitting, but you kept on going. Terrific!

- I can see a difference in your work compared to last week. Congratulations!

- I am so proud of the effort, and I hope you are too. It really paid off!

The timing of when to give praise is important. In making praise effective, a teacher should explicitly note the behavior as the reason for praise in as timely a manner as possible.

Praise is best connected to a process, rather than student intelligence. That is the basis of Dweck's research in her book *Mindset: The New Psychology of Success* (2007). She found "that praise for intelligence tended to put students in a fixed mindset (intelligence is fixed, and you have it), whereas praise for effort tended to put them in a growth mind-set (you're developing these skills because you're working hard)."[9] Of the two types of praise, Dweck notes, praise for student effort, such as *All that hard work and effort in completing the project paid off*, tends to improve student motivation.

Babemba Tribe

In *The Art of Forgiveness, Lovingkindness, and Peace*, Jack Kornfield describes an African forgiveness ritual:

> In the Babemba tribe of South Africa, when a person acts irresponsibly or unjustly, they are placed in the center of the village, alone and unfettered. All work ceases, and every man, woman, and child in the village gathers in a large circle around the accused individual. Then each person in the tribe speaks to the accused, one at a time, about all the good things the person

in the center of the circle has done in their lifetime. Every incident, every experience that can be recalled with any detail and accuracy is recounted. All positive attributes, good deeds, strengths, and kindnesses are recited carefully and at length. This tribal ceremony often lasts several days. At the end, the tribal circle is broken, a joyous celebration takes place, and the person is symbolically and literally welcomed back into the tribe.[10]

Our Tribe

Is this the way people are typically treated or cared for in our society? Punishment, shaming, and school suspension are the standard responses. One day, as I was visiting a high school campus, I came across a school administrator harshly reprimanding and shaming a student in front of a large group of his classmates. It was demeaning and mean-spirited. Yes, damage control had been done. The student's misbehaving stopped. Publicly, he was shamed in front of a whole group of his friends.

I thought: *After that verbal onslaught, that student may not show up at school tomorrow. He may not choose to come back to that school at all.*

How deep a reservoir of self-esteem and resilience might that student need to withstand that level of insult and public shame? How many mega-doses of honoring and praising might it take from teachers to restore that young person's self-image?

The Tribes Meet

As we've shared the Babemba Tribe story in our *Growth Heartset Educator Workshop*, teachers have taken this honoring practice back into their classrooms and tried it out for themselves. Eliana Farias, an outstanding former fifth grade teacher in Los Angeles and an EduCare program facilitator, recounts:

> So, the following week, I went back into my classroom, refreshed, renewed, and eager to apply some of the Heartset skills I had been presented, and sure enough, life provided an opportunity to do just that. Here came my Andrew. Every teacher has at least one in their class—that kid that has so much potential, whom you love, but works your every nerve from the time he arrives until the time he leaves.
>
> I had tried everything with him since the beginning of the year: taking recess away, taking away fun activities, assigning extra homework, writing ten times I will behave!, parent conferences, and on and on but all to no avail. He seemed to get worse, not better!
>
> One day, as I was walking to the chalkboard to write Drew's name on the board to take his recess time away for the umpteenth time, the Babemba Tribe story came back to mind, and I paused for a minute: Why not give it a try and see if it actually works? And so, I proceeded to tell my third grade class that we were going to play a new game, and Drew would go first. I explained and instructed them on what we would do, and they were

eager to participate in this cool new activity we were going to do, and they each wanted a turn.

I stood behind Drew in the circle, showing my presence and support of him and coached him to receive each praise/honor from his classmates. At first, he was a little nervous because 1) we had never done this before and 2) he didn't know what they would say. His classmates told him:

> "Thanks, Drew, because you were my first friend in kindergarten."
>
> "You shared your good crayons with me once and I really liked that!"
>
> "I remember once I was crying because no one wanted to play with me during recess, and you came over and started playing handball with me."
>
> "I like you, Drew, because you are nice and funny!"

I couldn't help but be touched by their heartfelt honesty and sincerity. I learned so much more about their past together and the interrelationships between all of them. The simple act of honoring and praising this child back into "sanity/normality" worked. The misbehaved, trouble-making Drew that began the circle wasn't the same Drew that ended that circle. He seemed pleasantly surprised after each comment and eager to hear what the next person had to say.

I don't know exactly how to describe what happened, but the best way would be to say that his spirit was touched, healed in some way, and made whole. Essentially, his love bucket filled. He had been honored and praised. He beamed with happiness and sported a new sense of purpose to connect more with his friends and our classroom. Drew knew he was loved, appreciated, wanted, and liked by all of us. And that meant the world to him.

Now, I wish I could tell you Drew never misbehaved ever again, but that wouldn't be true. He still did, but it was different because he was different, I was different, and our classroom was different. We had bonded like family, and we all felt the love in that circle. We continued doing our Love Circle, but we didn't wait until someone misbehaved to activate it. We did it each day at the end of the day as a way to go home happy and be excited about coming back to school the following day.

Opportunities to Praise Students

Judy Fujawa, in *Almost Everything You Need to Know About Early Childhood Education*, provides a list of optimal opportunities to praise students:[11]

1. When a student does better than his or her personal best.

2. When a student shows courage and perseverance when tackling a challenge.

3. When a student comforts or comes to the aid of a friend or classmate in need.

4. When a student completes a task or project.

5. When a student shows creativity in their words or actions.

6. When a student explores and follows through with an idea.

7. When a student takes on a new responsibility.

8. When a student leads by example.

Summary

Positively reinforcing, acknowledging, appreciating, and praising young people will encourage and inspire them to do their best and to keep growing and learning. Teaching them the value of praise shows them how important it is to see the best in themselves and in turn, the importance of acknowledging others. As students learn the power of honoring and praising, they more fully prepare themselves for success in school and a life of greater purpose and fulfillment.

Exercises For Educators/Parents

Journal

1. *Admiration Mirror*

What if what we see in others reflects the image that we hold for ourselves?

Choose someone you admire. Make this list in your journal.

- I admire *name*. The things I admire about him/her are: *fill in list*

- The things I admire about him/her are also true of me. Copy the same qualities you just wrote, starting each sentence with *I am*.

- The ways that I show those qualities in my life are: *fill in list*

2. *Praising*

Reflect on and then write about a time you honored or praised a child or another person (or someone praised you) and the positive impact it had on them, on you, and on your relationship.

Describe this event and your thoughts in your journal.

Compliments

Choose a day to give at least three people compliments today. Write down their names and what you said to them. Jot down how those compliments might also be true about you.

Then, look at yourself in the mirror and give yourself compliments out loud. How did that feel?

Exercises For Students/Children

Positive Feedback Cards

This activity works best after class members know one another fairly well. Ask each person to write their name in the upper corner of an index card, and then tell the group to place all the cards in the center pile. Instruct each person to draw a card and keep the result a secret. If they draw their own card, they should put it back in the pile and draw again.

Tell each student to write a thoughtful positive statement about the person named on their card and then put it back in the pile. Repeat this several times, and on the last turn, each person writes on the card and then reads the remarks out loud as warmly and sincerely as they can. The person named on the card receives a big round of applause.

Super Me Cape

Give a large piece of paper (a cape) to each student and have them write their name at the top. Under their name, have them write: *What's special about me?* Then, ask them to assist each other as they place the paper on their back with two pieces of tape.

Students move around the room, writing appreciative statements on each other's capes. After several minutes of milling and writing, everyone stops and takes off their cape. They sit in small circles and read out loud: *What's special about me?* and the answers written by their classmates. There's lots of applause and support as each person reads their strengths on their *Super Me* cape and shares their feelings if they wish.

Letter of Acknowledgment

Have students write a letter of appreciation to someone who's made a difference in their life. Ask them to mention how they were influenced by this person's actions, support, and love and express how this person has helped them move forward in life.

This exercise is effective for educators and parents as well.

Chapter Three

Listening From the Heart

Listening creates a holy silence. When you listen generously to people, they can hear truth in themselves, often for the first time. And in the silence of listening, you can know yourself in everyone.
— Rachel Naomi Remen, MD

Eddie

Eddie had cerebral palsy. Due to his CP, Eddie, an eleven-year-old, walked and ran with an awkward gait. Regardless, he had a fun-loving, joyful spirit. He didn't let his disabilities slow him down and was active in sports and camp activities.

During the summer after I completed high school, I was his camp counselor in upstate New York. Working with youngsters from the poorest neighborhoods in NYC, we had campers with a wide range of physical disabilities. Other campers would often make fun of Eddie, and he would seem to laugh it off.

The campers would always have a break after lunch and rest up before we went off and did our afternoon activities. One of the first days of camp during the rest period, Eddie walked over to me and asked, "Hey, can you help me with something?"

I said, "What's up?"

He replied, "Can you help me tie my shoelaces?

I said, "Sure."

From then on over the next two weeks each day during our cabin rest period, Eddie would sit next to me on the bed and learn how to bow his sneaker laces, cross over, and tie— practice, practice, practice. By the end of two weeks, he was thrilled. I was thrilled too. He could tie his shoes.

Returning to the city after summer. I got a call from his mom one day inviting me over to dinner. I gladly drove over to their small, low-income high-rise apartment in the Bronx. As we were sitting around the dinner table having conversation, I asked, "Mrs. Mandel, did you notice Eddie's new skill that he learned at summer camp?"

She said, "What do you mean?"

I said, "Did you notice how he can tie his shoes now?"

She looked at me. I looked at her and saw a funny look on her face. Eddie started smiling. She paused and with a gentle grin added, "Stu, Eddie came to camp knowing how to tie his shoes."

I said, "No way, he didn't, because we practiced that every day during rest period for twenty minutes."

Eddie was beaming and chuckling. She said to me, "You don't get it, do you, Stu?"

Puzzled, I replied, "What's going on?"

"Eddie doesn't have a dad," she answered, "and here you were with seven other kids in the cabin. Eddie thought: *What if I can get this caring, young counselor to spend time just with me for at least part of the day? I can con him into teaching me how to tie my shoes. That could work.*"

It sure did. It worked for Eddie, and looking back, it served as a turning point for me in my life. I realized that my simple act of kindness and heartfelt listening to a young boy who was reaching out for a friend could be monumental. That summer set me on the path to wanting to become a teacher. I experienced the transformational gift of empathetic listening and joyful caring for a young person.

> *To the world, you may just be one person, but to one person, you may be the world.*
> — Author unknown, but often attributed to Dr. Seuss

The Importance of Listening

We all want to be seen, heard, accepted, and known to another.

Truly listening and hearing another is a great tribute and expression of honoring another. Children flourish when heard. Intuitively, they realize that they are respected and worthy of being listened to.

> Children flourish when heard. Intuitively, they realize that they are respected and worthy of being listened to.

It is in listening—not trying to convince, advise, or instruct—that we create a safe space for others to be themselves, to express themselves. When that happens, there's a connection—a love—between people that can be profound. Taking the time and having the willingness to listen deeply is one of the highest forms of regard we can have for one another.

Listening Is a Skill

The skill of deep, empathetic listening takes time to learn and practice. It requires the desire and practice of connecting and listening to ourselves as well as to another. Our internal messages may come subtly as a sense of insight, intuition, or inner direction—a compassionate inner voice. As we nurture this habit of kinder, deeper listening to ourselves, then we can more readily be available for others.

Listening to ourselves is connected to self-acceptance and self-forgiveness. There may be times when we don't have the answers and we find ourselves impatient and wanting to know just what to do. At those times, we might choose to slow down, listen, and ask for guidance. In those levels of listening and trust, more can be revealed.

> As we cultivate that deeper inner wisdom of listening to ourselves, we strengthen our ability to empathetically listen.

This kind of listening may entail posing questions to ourselves and waiting over time to see where the answers come from. They may come from our dreams, journaling, reflection, or from the unfolding lessons of our ordinary life experiences. Those answers may come serendipitously from others. Listening requires letting go of the need to control, letting go of thinking we need to know all the answers right now.

What if, as we cultivate that deeper inner wisdom of listening to ourselves, we strengthen our ability to empathetically listen? As we carry an intention and become better equipped to ask, learn, and listen to ourselves, we become more available to others.

When We Don't Listen From the Heart

Sometimes we inadvertently shift away from heart listening when we are communicating with people in our lives. Jaya Ramchandani, in her article, "What Is Empathetic Listening?" lists ten common ways we often move away from listening from the heart.[12] She highlights:

- Giving advice—*I think you should know . . .*

- Explaining your situation—*But I didn't mean to . . .*

- Correcting the person—*Wait! I never said that!*

- Consoling the person—*You did the best you could . . .*

- Telling a story—*That reminds me of the time . . .*

- Shutting down feelings—*Cheer up. Don't be so mad.*

- Sympathizing—*Oh you poor thing . . .*

- Interrogating—*How come you did that?*

- Evaluating—*You're just too unrealistic.*

- One-Upping—*That's nothing. Listen to this!*

Levels of Listening

A model for understanding the various ways we can develop empathetic listening are Stephen Covey's *Levels of Listening*[13] as described in EduCare's *Heartset Education* workshops:

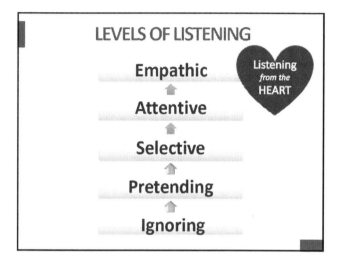

- **Ignoring** (distracted, looking away, turned off to what is being said)
- **Pretending** (might include nodding, smiling, but in fact not listening at all)
- **Selective** (involved if they agree with your point of view or if it's a topic you're interested in; otherwise tuned out)
- **Attentive** (sincerely interested paying attention and involved)
- **Empathic** (listening from the heart, connecting, seeking to understand, creating a safe space)

The Shift to Listening From the Heart

> *What does it mean to listen to a voice before it is*
> *spoken? It means making space for the other, being*
> *aware of the other, paying attention to the other, and*
> *honoring the other.*
>
> — Parker J. Palmer

Listening from the heart means expressing empathy by connecting to that place where we can feel what other people may be feeling, not just what they're saying. It involves listening to understand as well as listening to connect. A teachers, parents, or family members, sometimes we're so busy. We're distracted with our phones, devices, or our work. We don't take that time. Being mindful about how we do connect gives us an opportunity to truly listen.

To listen from the heart, we often need to pause and say to ourselves: *Well, if I'm not in that state of mind, if I am distracted, or if I have a lot going on, how do I change? How do I create that space right now in this moment to listen from the heart?*

P.E.A.C.E. and Empathetic Listening

The PEACE acronym below, as developed and taught by Margalit Ward, seminar leader and EduCare facilitator, highlights ways to shift to empathetic listening.

Patience: Slow down; be present. Breathe.

Empathy: Consider how they may be feeling, acceptance.

Attention: Give the person your full attention (eye contact, no distractions, nod, etc.).

Care and Curiosity: *People don't care how much you know, until they know how much you care.*

Engage: Participate in ways that let people know they've been heard. Reflect and ask questions. People know that you are interested and engaged when you are genuinely curious about what they are sharing.

Tips for Listening from the Heart

- Set an intention to listen and be present.

- Reach out and make time to listen.

- Put down your phone and distractions.

- Be mindful of your body language in person and online.

- Practice acceptance and letting go of judgments.

- Reflect back what you heard.

- Ask questions and just listen.

Susan Partnow, author of *The Five Practices of Compassionate Learning*, suggests that we "Offer listening as a gift, choosing to keep one's opinions, stories, and interpretations out of the way."[14]

Jaya Ramchandani writes:

> Empathetic listening is about really understanding the person who's talking to you. That means it goes

beyond active listening into the zone of non-judging and empathy. Non-judgment while you listen to others means you can truly hear them with an open mind. Empathy refers to emotionally connecting with another person through identification, compassion, understanding, feeling, and insight. Empathetic listening is needed most when someone needs to be seen and heard.[15]

Empathetic listening is being present and listening from the heart. Empathetic listening lets others know you sincerely care. Its effect is profound. As Rachel Naomi Remen so wisely states, "A loving silence often has far more power to heal and to connect than the most well-intentioned words."[16]

Summary

Deep, compassionate listening is one of the greatest gifts we can give to another, to let others know we recognize them just the way they are—their strengths, weaknesses, uncertainties, burdens, and their joys. They do not need to change or follow our advice. To accept others just as they are is a powerful expression of honoring another. By deepening our listening skills and creating a space for each of us to be just as we are, we dynamically expand our *Heartset* in service to others and ourselves.

> Empathetic listening is being present and listening from the heart.

Exercise For Educators/Parents

Journal

Listening to Yourself

Complete the following statements in your journal as many times as you wish. After each complete statement, take a moment to jot down any specific memories that may come to mind.

1. *I feel challenged when* . . . (I'm tired; I don't feel well physically; people don't listen, etc.)

2. *I feel supported when* . . . (I get help in the kitchen and with housework; I feel heard; I connect to, etc.)

3. *Some things I can I do to support myself better are* . . . (get ready for bed earlier; choose time to talk to others when they'll be more receptive; drink more water; take breaks, etc.)

Centering for Listening

- Reflect on your day. Were there times that you *checked out* when someone was talking to you? Try to describe your feelings at that moment. Were you frustrated, overwhelmed, bored, judgmental, tired, or angry?

- Ask yourself what you could have done in this moment to re-engage with the speaker and truly listen. Breathe deeply? Put down your phone/pen/work? Schedule a time to speak when you were not overwhelmed with tasks?

- Do you have a time of day when you find it difficult to focus on what others are saying (the end of a long day)? What brief action or mind shift can you take to help retain your ability to listen? A quick walk? Deep breathing? A healthy snack to keep your energy levels up?

- Practice silently honoring the individual and listen for what they may be teaching you—patience? Make a note and try to incorporate this into your daily routine.

Listening to Others

Complete the following statements with a partner. When your partner is speaking, listen from the heart, practicing empathy in silence.

1. Someone I appreciate in my life is _____, because . . .

2. Some things I appreciate about myself are_____, because . . .

Family/Group Talk

This exercise provides an opportunity for each member to be heard and to practice deep listening from the heart with the other members. Give each person a chance to complete the following sentences without anyone else saying anything (i.e., agreeing, denying, making comments, etc.) Also, refrain from nonverbal disagreements as well, such as shaking heads, sighing, crossing arms, or appearing distracted.

This is a special time to speak and hear what is true for you and others. Everyone will have a chance to complete the selected sentence stem with each family member, and then it will be the next person's turn. Remember, feedback is best received when delivered in an honest and loving way. Use this time to share your caring with each other. This can be done with one question per day or per week.

1. *What I appreciate about you is . . .*

2. *What I need more of from you is . . .*

3. *What I need less of from you is . . .*

4. *What I'd like for us to do less of is . . .*

5. *What I'd like for us to do more of is . . .*

6. *Something I've never told you is . . .*

7. *Something I'd like to hear from you is . . .*

The person receiving this feedback will now say to the person who delivered the statement what it is they really wanted to hear.

Exercises For Students/Children

You listen with only one purpose: to help him or her to empty their heart. Even if he or she says things that are full of wrong perceptions, full of bitterness, you are still capable of continuing to listen with compassion.

— Thich Nhat Hanh

Heart Talks (also known as *Trust Circles* in the book *Making the Best of Me*)

Purpose:

- To introduce a tool for effective and caring communication

- To promote awareness of the importance of a safe place to share

- To build group cohesiveness, trust, and support

Procedure:

1. Discuss with the class times when they felt safe confiding in someone they could trust. Also discuss times when others confided in them. Use your personal examples. Review how valuable it can be for the class to create a *safe place* within their group for talking about things in a deeper, more honest way. Indicate that this activity is about creating a caring and safe place for sharing from that deeper, more *real* place from inside each of us.

2. Review the guidelines for leading a Heart Talk:

   a. One person speaks at a time. Everyone else listens without comments, side talking, or interruptions. Discourage nonverbal cues as well, such as shaking heads, heavy sighing, crossing arms, looking away as if disinterested, etc. Can introduce a *talking stick* or item that is passed around the circle and only the person holding the *stick* is permitted to speak. It can be a meaningful or an impromptu item—e.g., a heart shaped cutout, stuffed toy, pencil, stick, pine cone, seashell, or one the group selects that may illicit caring or peace.

   b. When the first person is done, the next person (either to the right or to the left) begins.

   c. Everyone is encouraged to blend honesty and personal responsibility in their sharing. Rather than statements of blaming others, students are to practice using "I" statements.

   d. Everything that is said is kept confidential in the group.

   e. Though everyone is encouraged to talk, it is okay for someone to pass when it is their turn in the circle.

   f. The speaker is encouraged to make eye contact with others in the group. The group supports each person by just listening.

g. Everyone's comments are accepted. There is no need for anyone to contest or rebut someone's point of view.

3. Have the students arrange their chairs in a circle. It is best to set aside all desks and tables. Later, after students are familiar with this technique, they can form small trust circles.

4. It is fine for the leader to go first to demonstrate willingness to be vulnerable and risk. This can set the tone for the Heart Talk. Example: What is your favorite sport or hobby and why? What is something you wish adults would do differently? What was your most embarrassing moment?

5. Begin the Heart Talk with someone who volunteers to start.

Possible topics for Heart Talks are:

- Who do you appreciate the most in your life and why?

- If you could change one thing about yourself, what would it be and why?

- Describe a time when you did something courageous/ kind.

- How would you want the world to be different for your children?

- How do you "push" your parents' buttons?

- If your friend were going to describe all the great things about you, what would he/she say?

- What qualities do you look for in a friend?

- If you could teach everyone in the world one thing, what would it be?

Discussion:

Discuss the merits of this type of communication. Remind students that it is not a time to teach or get information, but a time to share in a safe and relaxed atmosphere. It is a time to seek to understand.

Heart Seat (from *Making the Best of Me*)

Purpose:

- To give each person an opportunity to talk honestly, respectfully, and with caring to each member of the group

- To let each person's words be heard

- To practice listening

- To build group trust

Procedure:

1. Post some appropriate partial sentences on the board. Here are some suggestions:

    What I like or appreciate about you is . . .

    One thing I think you offer to this class is . . .

One thing that I want to thank you for is . . .

The way I think I could be more helpful to you is . . .

What I respect about you is . . .

2. Divide the class into small groups (6–8 students).

3. Ask who wants to go first and have them sit in a chair which will be designated the *heart seat*. The only job of the person in the *heart seat* is to listen and receive feedback.

4. The group members take turns giving feedback by completing the first sentence.

5. After each member has taken a turn giving feedback, then it is another member's turn to sit in the *heart seat* and receive the caring communication.

6. Repeat this process until everyone has had their turn.

Tell the students:

• When you are in the *heart seat*, just listen without answering back or making comments.

• Make eye contact as you both deliver and receive your communications.

• Practice blending honesty and caring in your communication.

• Have fun and allow the specialness of your group to build.

Chapter Four

The Power of Choice—*Personal Responsibility*

Everything can be taken from a man but one thing:
the last of the human freedoms—to choose one's
attitude in any given set of circumstances,
to choose one's own way.

— Viktor Frankl

Power and Viktor Frankl

When we think of power in this world, we may think of those who have positions of authority, control, physical strength, status, or wealth. What if authentic personal power could be measured in an entirely different way? What if power at the truest level is really the power of our choice at any moment, under any circumstance, and any condition?

Life circumstances do not need to be the cause for negative reactions and attitudes. The ultimate choice we all have is the choice of

> The ultimate choice we all have is the choice of our attitude at any moment.

our attitude at any moment. Rather than resorting to blaming and complaining as the easy way out of owning our power to choose, we can respond to life with wise and self-honoring decisions.

Stunning examples of tremendous personal power shine through the lives of inspiring people who have demonstrated great courage and compassion in the midst of extreme hardship. One in particular was Viktor Frankl who endured the tortures of concentration camps and the horrors of imprisonment but never lost his purpose in life. An entry in the blog *The Power of Choice: Freedom Over Circumstances* depicts Frankl's incredible strength of purpose:

> I dare say that few of us will undergo the horrors that Viktor (Frankl) experienced in the death camps. Yet in the midst of that situation, he realized his true freedom. The power to choose his attitude. In fact, he said that though the Nazis could take everything from him, they could not take away this: his power to choose his response to them. [17]

Frankl shared his food, his clothing, and his kindness with his fellow prisoners. He endured years of torture and the loss of those closest to him. He amazingly continued to choose generosity, gratitude, hope, and a deep purpose for life that kept him alive in the midst of the most horrific of circumstances.

My Choice

I began teaching history and math at Audubon Middle School in the heart of South Los Angeles. I was a rookie teacher in the LA Unified School District, full of enthusiasm and hoping to have my students see themselves and their lives as full of wonderful possibilities.

Walking into other classrooms, I would see some teachers sitting behind a desk, newspaper slapped right in front of their face with their students doing some boring worksheets or with heads down on their desks. The teacher was disconnected. Not engaged at all. As I left the classrooms, I would question myself: *Will that be me? Is that how I am going to be as a teacher?* And more importantly: *Is that the way young people should be taught?*

It was at that point I decided I was going to do it differently. I simply knew it was necessary. Our young people were too important. They deserved to receive more than what they were getting from these teachers.

It was kind of a turning point for me. I knew what type of teacher I wanted to become—and what kind of teacher I *didn't* want to be.

I immersed myself in my personal growth, attending numerous seminars and workshops. I began to put together an outline of the type of education my students truly needed. I started experimenting with what I was learning and incorporating the necessary principles and concepts into my lessons with seventh and eighth graders. I used creative visualizations, affirmations, journal writing, and reflective learning. I added conversations with a partner, circling together in small groups, fostering discussion of feelings, values, and the *glows* and *grows* of what was going on in our lives.

I saw my kids getting in touch with who they were and connecting in deeper ways with each other. Their self-worth grew. Their motivation for learning was sparking. Teachers would drop in and tell me that these students were doing better in their classrooms since they enrolled in my elective class.

I was witnessing the value of another sort of education, an education of self-awareness, of personal meaning. This is what I earnestly wanted for my students.

Strawberry Mansion High School (1990)

I was facilitating an EduCare ACE Program for a group of about 120 students in one of the tougher high schools in the area, located in one of the poorest neighborhoods in Philadelphia. We were crowded together in a large and bare multipurpose room at this rundown relic of a high school. Many of the participating students didn't care to be at school, let alone attend a required student success program. On day two of our three-day program, I started the morning by telling the packed room of students, "Guess what? You don't have to be here today. You don't have to attend the program if you don't want to."

I purposely paused, looked around, and waited to see what type of response that might elicit. The room became pretty quiet. Students started looking to one another, some smiling and gesturing. Then one student, a tall athletic-looking young man, stood up and made his way to the center aisle. He slowly began to walk toward the back exit of the room. Along the way, he would pause at times and look back at me expecting a response. I would calmly remind him, "It's up to you. You can leave or you can stay." He continued toward the door, walking slower and slower, glancing back at me occasionally to see what I was going to do.

"No, it's up to you," I told him. "However, think about what the consequences will be once you walk out the door."

Close to the door, he stopped, turned around, and disgruntledly started making his way back to his seat. "Well, since you are making me stay, I'll stay."

I challenged him, "No, you're free to go. It's up to you."

He shrugged and came back to his chair, sat down, and said, "Okay. I'm here since you are making me stay. I get it."

Once again, I told him, "No, it's been up to you. But now that you returned and are in your seat, you have another choice." I paused. "What do you want to do now?"

He had no clue what I was driving at, and that was okay with me. I asked him why he turned around and came back to his seat, rather than walk out the door. He replied, "Oh, if I walked out, I'd probably get caught by the dean and suspended. And if just sit here, I can hang out and be bored."

"I get it," I said. "So you made your choice."

He looked at me, puzzled. I told him, "Guess what? Now you have another choice. What do you want to have happen now that you are here? Boredom or something else? That will be your next choice."

Wonderfully enough, he started to choose to participate more fully throughout the next two days. It was on *him* from the start. He gained that ever-present power of choice.

Turning Point Choices

In approaching life-changing choices, what does it take to stop and become aware of what is in front of us? We may not know we are facing a choice that is a turning point. This is where the inclination to be mindful, to pause, and to listen deeply to our own intuition is the best course of action. Patience is an asset. Being honest in dealing with our doubt or facing our fear of making a choice and taking action—or choosing not to act—is required.

As Nick Segal writes in his book, *On Your Terms*: "Consider: if you never make a decision, decisions will keep being made for you. And that is not a model for a living that breeds success." He describes it as "radical responsibility" and emphasizes that we all get to "call the shots" once we choose to. He shares that "the more you stay vigilant and diligent in your journey to your vision . . . [you] create a life that you love."[18]

Be Willing to Fail

Part of choosing is being open to failing, to picking ourselves up, and to moving on. It is human to make mistakes, but how we choose to deal with our mistakes, as well as our willingness to fail, will allow us to succeed in the future. The choice to be less than perfect, to make mistakes, is a life-affirming choice.

What do little infants do when learning to walk? They fall. Then what? They get up and try again, only to fall once more. Have you ever heard an infant call this out after falling: *Guess what? I'm never gonna try walking again in my life. I give up.*

Even if babies could talk, you wouldn't hear them say that. They just stand up and fall down repeatedly in the adventure of learning how to walk. Your attitudes and choices about your mistakes have a lot to do with their effect on you.

Have you heard the saying: *What if mistakes are learning opportunities cleverly disguised as problems?* Mistakes tell you what you need to know. If a student spells a particular word incorrectly on a spelling test, this tells them they need to study that word some more. Thomas Edison made over 1000 mistakes before he created the lightbulb. Good thing for us he didn't quit.

It's been said that how we choose to face the problems in our lives determines if those problems are *stumbling blocks* or *opportunities.* Mistakes can be opportunities for our advancement, learning, and growth. Drs. Ron and Mary Hulnick, of the University of Santa Monica, in their book, *Loyalty To Your Soul: The Heart of Spiritual Psychology,* wisely state that "how you relate to an issue is the issue, and how you relate to yourself while you go through an issue is the issue."[19]

Choosing Not to Choose

The nimbleness, the agility, and the awareness to realize that our choices are all at hand gives us great freedom, power, and ability to respond.

One of the choices that people often make is to believe they have no personal power, that the world is in charge, and there's not much they can do about it. They may consider themselves victims, victimized by the world or by the situation they find themselves in. No doubt, each of us at times will face unjust and unfair circumstances. How we respond to those situations and circumstances is the root of the power of our choice.

When we deny our personal ability to respond, we may feel it is because others *make us* do things. Much like that student at Strawberry Mansion High School in Philadelphia, we can hide behind the storyline, saying, *I'm just a kid*, *I'm just one teacher*, or *I'm just his/her parent.*

What can I do? The power of one individual is immeasurable. We can see it in our ever-changing world when social injustices and inequities are being called out. There is power in speaking out. The collective ability of those who choose to respond can have great impact.

We Always Have a Choice

What if we could see that we have choices in every situation?

It's much easier to have tunnel vision and feel as if we have no choice at all. It's easier to *blame and complain*, pointing fingers elsewhere.

Mark Samuel and Sophie Chiche describe this pattern well in their book, *The Power of Personal Accountability*. It is outlined in their *Personal Accountability Model*. It starts when

. . . a situation comes up and it's usually a challenging one. Based on your intention, you have a choice regarding how to respond. When you take the victim road, you ignore the problem, deny your involvement in it, and eventually blame someone else. Then, you visualize, you rationalize, and you justify why another person should take care of it and resist any attempt that others may make to get you involved. Finally, you hide to avoid dealing with it.[20]

We may not always see the choices we have in the situations that occur in life, but we always have them. We can always choose how we respond. Blaming and complaining are sure signs of not taking personal responsibility.

Candace

In the spring of 1997, my lovely wife was diagnosed with bone cancer. I suddenly felt as if my whole world was going to fall apart. Though I wanted to keep a strong appearance, I soon dropped into a deep depression. I feared the worst in what was to come, for my wife, for me, and for our son, Jeff.

At first, I wasn't thinking about my choices. I was just stuck in the depth of sadness

> Blaming and complaining are sure signs of not taking personal responsibility.

and overwhelm. My mind was running wild with worst-case scenarios. My emotions followed the downward spiral of my fearful thinking. I had little awareness that I could take any control. Fortunately, in my willingness to consider stepping past heavy feelings of victimhood, I gradually was able to lift into a place of hope, along with the prospect of personal empowerment.

One of the most dynamic catalysts for my change was my wife, Candace, when I saw the way she was responding to her own diagnosis. She was determined, optimistic, proactive, and diligently looking with me for the medical support that would get her through. It would have been easy for her to let fear and worry run the show. But she didn't.

We looked for the best of doctors who carried the medical experience, the expertise, and the *heartset* of optimism and faith. We landed on an amazing orthopedic oncologist who headed our medical team. At one of our first appointments, he said something to us that jolted me out of my depression and turned my life around. After a careful examination of Candace's case, he looked at us and said, "Candace and Stu, I want you to know that you are about to enter into the most challenging and hardest year ever. Candace, there will be many series of chemo treatments and all the painful effects afterwards. They'll be weeks in the hospital. But I also want you to know that I see a year from now you, Candace, will be walking down the sidewalks here in Los Angeles. When people look at you, who they will see is one beautiful, radiant woman." In that moment, I knew where the doctor's power of choice was, and I knew where mine was to be as well.

The power of that choice of positivity and hope was a timely call for me to take charge of my attitude, my thoughts, and my feelings. It was a tremendously challenging year for Candace and our family, as well as all the wonderful friends around us.

So many miracles of support, comfort, and reassurance came forward.

As we courageously took the difficult steps we needed to take, we knew we had the will to keep moving forward. We moved on the principle that *the willingness to do creates the ability to do.* Sometimes for me it was just taking the next breath or handling the sudden setbacks that kept appearing. Getting the pain medications' level right. Dealing with the fear that the cancer may have moved to her brain. Dreading the thought that she may be receiving never-ending rounds of chemo.

Now, more than twenty-four years later, I get to walk down the city sidewalks alongside a beautiful and radiant woman, my wife, Candace. The power of our choices has been boosted by the grandeur of our faith and the enormity of our gratefulness.

The Power to Choose—Attitudes, Focus, and Actions

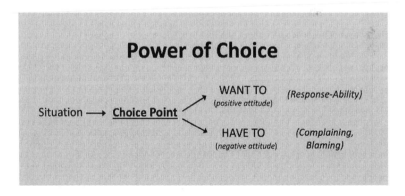

We strip ourselves of our power when we choose a fixed mindset of looking at life as if we have been loaded down with *have-tos.* A *have-to* is something you do and don't enjoy doing—but you do it anyway. It is often accompanied by displeasure, a lack of desire, and little motivation. It may also be accompanied by a steady stream of complaining and blaming.

The opposite of choosing a *have to* attitude is choosing a *want to* attitude. The concrete act of actually choosing is of itself a neutral act. After we decide that we are going to choose to do—or not do—something, we instantaneously make a second internal choice—the choice of *attitude*.

Moving from *I have to* to *I choose to* is an enormously empowering choice. Think about mornings when you wake up and you know you get to start a vacation or a well-anticipated fun day. The attitude and associated feeling is one of *I want to get up; I want to start this day.*

Compare that to the attitude we choose when it's time to turn off the alarm on the morning of a day of work that we dread. It is the same hour of the morning, and it's the same alarm clock. Who's in charge of how we get out of bed? Who is responsible for making it a *want to* or a *have to?*

What if those feelings of *oh no, another dreaded day* are actually moments of awareness that are opportunities for choosing something different, for choosing a positive attitude and a growth mindset? With a positive attitude, we can switch that victimized feeling to a position of power: *How fortunate I am. I get to go to work.*

The power of choice opens the door to taking advantage of the amazing opportunities that life situations and circumstances provide us with. We can choose to make empowering and self-honoring responses.

The attitude of gratitude is perhaps one of the most self-empowering choices. To be grateful for all that comes forward in our life, regardless of if we labeled it *a good thing* or *a bad thing*. To accept it all as perhaps *perfect*—in that it provides stunning, though often difficult, opportunities to handle life events in ways that teach and empower us.

We also get to choose where we place our focus, intentions, and self-talk. For example, as Carly Simon's popular song points out, we can redirect our focus because we ". . . haven't got time for the pain." That redirect of our mental and resulting emotional attention can be a conscious choice. It is simply underscored in Peter McWilliams and John-Roger's book title: *We Can't Afford the Luxury of a Negative Thought*. Where do we choose our focus, attention, and intention—on relentless fear and worry? Or on hope, joy, opportunities, and positive outcomes?

Along with attitude and focus, we also get to choose, regardless of the circumstances and situations that we face, our actual responses and behaviors. At

> The attitude of gratitude is perhaps one of the most self-empowering choices.

every moment, we can do our best to move from a blaming and complaining *have to* stance, to self-serving and uplifting choices of positive attitude, focus, and action. Though not always easy, this is response-ability—our ability to respond—at its finest. Practicing it may offer a challenge; yet it holds the utmost reward.

*Gratitude is the key to positive focus, which leads to
positive choices that lead to positive results.*

— John Morton, educator and author

Summary

The ultimate freedom and power we each have is to take responsibility on many levels simultaneously—responsibility for our feelings, our thoughts, and our actions. Nothing empowers us more than the responsibility we take for the choices we make moment to moment in our lives. No one can take that authority away from us. We can disempower ourselves, however, by simply giving that power away. It happens when we lose the belief that we are actually always in charge. That's our choice too.

Choosing personal responsibility leads to practicing a positive attitude, wiser decision making, and more effective problem solving. The *blaming habit* can then be replaced by a life enriched with increased clarity, self-trust, and inner freedom. The result is greater peace, personal balance, and empowerment.

Exercise For Educators/Parents

Journal

Have-Tos:

We disempower ourselves when we choose the mindset of looking at our lives as if we have been loaded down with *have-tos*. What is a *have-to?* As we discussed in this chapter, it is something you do and don't enjoy doing—but you do it anyway. We often complain about and blame others for our *have-tos*.

Answer the following questions in your journal:

- What are some of your *have-tos?*

- Who do you tell yourself *makes you* do your *have-tos?* Where do you point your finger?

- What is the story line that you use to think of yourself as a *victim*—a person with no choices—in your life?

- How might you take greater *response*-ability?

- What are actions you might take to promote responsibility in your classroom, school, workplace, and home?

Exercises For Students/Children

Share the *Power* = *Choice* graphic with students. Discuss the difference between a *have-to* mentality and a *choose-to* mindset. Then consider the following topics for a Learning Conversation with your students (or create a topic of your own).

1. Talk about a situation in which you felt like you had no choice.

   Examples:

   > *When my parents/brother/sister/ . . .*

   > *When my teachers . . .*

   > *When my friends . . .*

   > *In the hall at school, on the practice field, in the lunchroom . . .*

2. How might you turn a *have-to* to a *choose-to*? What thoughts might help you? What might you choose to do differently, to take on your ability to respond, your *response*-ability?

Chapter Five

Resolving Conflict

It's not you versus me. It's you and me versus the problem. The problem is the problem . . . Don't bring your adversaries to their knees— bring them to the table.
— Colman McCarthy, educator and journalist

What does conflict mean to you?

Take a moment to complete this sentence:

Conflict means . . .

For some, conflict may mean arguing, upset, discord, strife, fighting, abuse, or death. For others, it may mean challenge, opportunity, learning, growth, strengthening, or mastery. The perspective on how we perceive *conflicts* within us and around us sets the stage for how we then approach and handle them.

Now complete this sentence:

I experience conflict when . . .

(I'm afraid, confused, angry, irritated, not getting my way, etc.)

There are many different forms of conflict, including:

- Physical conflict: ownership, territorial, power struggles, fights, warfare

- Emotional conflict: annoyance, frustration, hurts, guilt, resentment

- Mental conflict: uncertainty, doubt, indecision, confusion

Conflict happens on many levels inside relationships, families, organizations, communities, societies, and nations.

And, it is ever-present within ourselves. We can expect a conflict will be at our doorstep regularly throughout our lives. We can choose to view conflict as a roadblock or as an opportunity for learning and growth.

The Starting Point

What if we can define conflict as something other than a menacing problem to avoid or win over?

Take some time to consider the following questions:

1. What if conflict is an opportunity for learning and growth?

> We can choose to view conflict as a roadblock or as an opportunity for learning and growth.

2. What if all conflicts in relationships—all conflicts, actually—are primarily based on the relationship we have with ourselves?

3. What if our experiences outside ourselves mirror the experiences (including conflict) within ourselves?

4. What if how we're relating to ourselves—and our own inner discord—is often projected outward in ways that places us in conflict with what shows up in our worlds?

Understanding the inner dimensions of our own conflicts sheds light on the dynamics of how we experience conflict in our relationships and in the world around us. It assists us in developing methods to resolve conflict in cooperative, peaceful, and educational ways, bringing greater balance and clarity to our lives. It also sets the stage for developing effective communication techniques for conflict resolution.

Years ago, I participated in a seminar where they shared a claim that caught my attention: *Participate in this course and wake up every day with the one you love.* The choice to wake up with the one I love (me) or the one I am in conflict with (also me) rests with me. It spoke to me that we are the ones who can create harmonious relationships or relationships full of distress and conflict. It's in our hands as part of the power of our choice. The first step is to acknowledge the possibility that we create, promote, or allow the conflicts we experience.

> The stirring of conflict begins with a basic human desire to want to be right.

Sources of Conflict

> *Nobody can bring you peace but yourself.*
> — Ralph Waldo Emerson

The stirring of conflict begins with a basic human desire to want to be right. This striving to prove ourselves *in the right* seems to justify our identity or self-worth. Sometimes, we seem to think: *I'd rather be right than happy*, and we will go a long way to prove ourselves right and others wrong. In this quest to build up our *rightness*—aka righteousness—we stack on a litany of expectations, *shoulds*, and ensuing judgments upon others and ourselves.

When others—and ourselves—don't measure up to these expectations and fall short, things move out of joint and grow discordant, and then we are in conflict. *Of course*, we think, *it must be someone else's fault. They just didn't do it my way.*

Conflicts are stirred up around big things and often seemingly little things. They typically occur whenever people disagree over their values, motivations, perceptions, ideas, or desires. Sometimes these differences seem petty, but when a conflict sparks strong reactions, a deep personal need is often at the core. These needs that are being threatened can include the need to feel safe, respected, or valued. They may reflect a need for greater closeness and intimacy. The ensuing upset and emotions often stem from the desire to be in control or to want things our own way, which of course is the *right and proper way.*[21]

Have you noticed that some of us avoid conflict at all costs while others enjoy creating as much conflict as possible? Discord may be sought as a technique for gaining power, authority, or control over others and can be viewed from a global perspective or closer to home in our relationships, with our families, in our organizations, and with colleagues.

A Story: Aye, Aye, Captain!

Through the years, my wife Candace and I, like many other couples, would have disagreements about petty things, though they may not have seemed petty at the time—how to furnish a room, to manage our money, or where to go out for dinner. Sound familiar? As our interactions started to heat up, we would catch ourselves in the moment and start to smile, thinking: *Here we are again.* Each of us wanted to be right. We were making a case for our opinions or desires while discrediting the other person's case.

As we grew aware of the insidious trap of righteousness, we turned to humor to move through our melodrama. When one of us would catch the other demanding their position was *right*, we played a game of standing at attention and saluting them with the phrase "Aye, aye, Captain!" Smiles turned to laughs, defusing our investment in needing to be the winner in this debate. We reversed *I'd rather be right than happy* to *We'd rather be happy than right.*

People often choose to be right over getting along with one another. What's the price we pay in ourselves and in our relationships for this strong desire to be right at all costs? Consider this well-known phrase: *Yes, they were dead right.* The cost to our relationships and even to our own health and well-being is too high.

We might submerge ourselves in conflict as a way of avoiding responsibility for showing up in our lives. Not making decisions, not choosing to step away, to communicate, or resolve a conflict is an easy way out. Then we can point the finger of responsibility somewhere else, claiming there was nothing we could do. Undermining and reinforcing emerging conflicts are ways to fall into victimhood and this fixed mindset of *I don't have any control.*

Conflicts can be warning signals to step in and take charge. To discover what we need to do to help resolve the conflict for ourselves and for others is possible.

The Nature of Conflict

Conflict is part of a natural process. It's how we respond to conflict that is the issue, not the conflict itself.

As shared in Insight Seminars, people typically respond to conflict by:

1. Running from it (direct avoidance/flight)

2. Struggling or fighting it, analyzing it (paralysis by analysis)

3. Slipping past it (the sophisticated, slippery, sidestep approach)

4. Facing it full on

> Conflict is part of a natural process. It's how we respond to conflict that is the issue, not the conflict itself.

By sitting in conflict and experiencing it fully, we can then ask ourselves: *What if I had a part in bringing this about?* And if that's the case: *What if I have the ability to either increase this conflict or lessen it?* In this way, conflict becomes a teacher, a strengthener, and even a friend as we face it and practice mastering it.

We can consider conflicts both internally and externally. Conflicts with ourselves regularly revolve around *should I or shouldn't I do it, what's right or wrong, or what I did or didn't do.* The conflicts we have in our relationships with others may mirror in many ways the conflicts we are having with ourselves.

Our conflicts "out there" often mirror the conflicts we're having inside ourselves.

In my seventh grade history classes, there were days when I would tell my students I wasn't having the best of days. I was sensitive, and the slightest craziness from them would throw me off. I thought my imbalance was because of them and their acting out and not following my standards.

The truth of the matter was the upset I was experiencing with my students was proportional to the imbalance I was experiencing within myself. I started to realize that the person who needed a *time out* was not one of my students, but me. I would hear myself wisely telling my students to go easy on me—to not push my buttons as I was having a tough day and not in the best of moods. It would have been easy to place the reason for the conflict on them and their behavior instead of acknowledging it had a lot to do with what was happening inside of me. It became an opportunity to be honest with myself and with them, to be more forgiving of us both, and to gently guide myself back into greater balance.

Remember: Conflicts within ourselves will often be projected as conflicts around us. How we respond to life and our conflicts is the issue. Our response is always in our hands.

Perspective

> *We don't see things as they are; we see things as WE ARE.*
> — Anais Nin, author

We bring our unique perspective, experience, and beliefs to every interaction and situation. So before we judge or assume, there is an opportunity to understand each other's perspectives and experiences.

Perspectives / Points of View

It is hard at times to listen to and consider ideas and opinions you disagree with.

Are these thoughts familiar?

How could they possibly think that way?

That's crazy!

What's wrong with them?

What's wrong? Maybe nothing. What's wrong through one person's eyes is unquestionably right through another's. And here we find ourselves again, with our desires to be right preventing us from considering different points of view. We find ourselves triggered, our own emotions rising to the surface, sometimes strongly.

Let's explore how to approach these *wrong* points of view that trigger us and disturb our peace. We need to hold an honest intention to surrender the need to always be in the right. This sincere willingness to let go of strongly held positions leads to greater self-awareness, to understanding rather than judging, and to openly considering and understanding others' perspectives and points of view. The awareness of what triggers us helps us choose a different response in the moment. We can choose a response that supports greater understanding, balance, and peace.

Trauma and Stressors

We would be remiss if we did not mention trauma at this point in our discussion. We know it has a huge impact on how people respond to conflict. Our students bring their past traumas into our classrooms, and we carry our traumas with us as well. These experiences and the triggers they produce are often deeply buried.

So what triggers us? What are the things that disturb our peace so much that we righteously justify our upset at all costs? What are the triggers that stand in the way of us being more in balance and effective?

Many of us have dealt with an uptick in conflict as we have stayed at home throughout the recent pandemic. Families are overwhelmed, with little or no time to ourselves. We can be triggered even more than usual when we are stressed, and we may be dealing with even more stressors as we transition back into our schools, our workplaces—into a new normal. *Heartset* Skills are needed now more than ever.

What Can We Do?

Our willingness to reflect and look at our part in creating, promoting, or allowing conflicts goes a long way. We can accept that conflict is present. We may not like, approve, or condone it, but we need to recognize when it is here. Once we recognize it, we can realize an opportunity to learn instead of acting quickly to deflect the discord or reactively respond.

Checking in to see where the conflict resides inside of us is essential.

- Is it a judgment I have placed against another or myself?

- Is it an expectation of how they or I should behave differently?

- Is it a need to be right and make someone else wrong, to build myself up due to a lack of self-worth or self-value?

Awareness, acceptance, self-inquiry, and personal responsibility (ownership) are the important steps in moving through our self-damaging storyboards of conflict. Part of the acceptance process is to allow for and invite various points of view.

Resolving Conflict in Cooperative, Peaceful, and Educational Ways

- Start with yourself—take personal responsibility.

- Consider that you always have the power to choose your response, attitude, and perspective.

- Develop self-awareness, mindfulness, and inner balance.

- Identify judgements—the *shoulds*—you're placing on others and yourself.

- Find opportunities for greater acceptance, honesty, communication, forgiveness, empathy, and understanding.

There Can Be Peace

In August 1999, about 120 Jewish, Arab, and Druze teachers from four separate elementary and junior high schools in Israel came together through EduCare's ACE Teacher Institute, to learn how to integrate the ACE Program into their classes. For many Jewish, Arab, and Druze teachers, it was their first time training together in this way. The tension was high to say the least. However, once each person realized their common interest—the welfare of the children—the tension began to dissipate. It even became joyful and fun.

Two months later, in October, the first of a series of three-day ACE Student Workshops began. About eighty-five wonderful, enthusiastic Israeli Arab fifth graders and their teachers and counselors came together in a modern community center in Umm al-Fahm, an impoverished Arab town on the outskirts of Haifa.

We experienced several days of wonderful interactions between students, teachers, and facilitators. However, toward the end of the third day, we were presented with a challenge that almost ended this project for good. It seems that Aviva, the Israeli woman who was head of EduCare Israel, had arranged a meeting with the Arab town mayor. When she learned he was considered by the Israeli government to be an active political extremist, she canceled the meeting. The mayor was deeply insulted. He was considering canceling the program before it was off the ground.

At midday on the last day of the student workshop, the principal told us that the students would be going home immediately unless we agreed to see the mayor, without Aviva. We wanted to meet the mayor; however, we also believed it was critical to the program for Aviva to be there. It was a stalemate. The principal was upset, and his reputation was on the line.

The good news was that the Arab teachers and principal had seen what the ACE Program was already accomplishing with their kids, and they loved it. The principal pulled his dozen teachers aside to confer. Our little group stood about fifteen feet away from them, also trying to figure out what to do.

I asked for inner guidance, and then listened for an answer. The solution was near—fifteen feet away to be exact. We Jewish EduCare staffers could walk those fifteen feet over to the teacher group and join them. We could work this out, but only if we worked together. We took one step, and then another.

It was marvelous. Before we knew it, we were brainstorming. We all loved the kids and the program, and we kept that at the heart of our talking—not the politics, not the hurt feelings, not the petty egos—but the kids and our desire to cooperate. Within minutes, we had the solution. Two of the male Arab teachers said, "Stu, you and the two of us, let us go first and speak with the mayor. Let us tell him that Aviva comes in forgiveness, and let us ask him to allow her to come with us all to tell him about the great ACE Program and to have it continue throughout the year in our school." It was a gem.

The men and I went to the mayor's office. He was traditional in his manner, very gracious. I expressed to the mayor our appreciation for hosting ACE in his town; the Arab teachers spoke up and praised ACE. Then one of them quietly approached the mayor and asked him to allow Aviva to visit.

The mayor became thoughtful. We held our breath. He paused, then nodded his approval.

Within minutes, Aviva and the women teachers arrived. Kind words were shared, apologies were tendered and accepted, and the mayor gave us his blessings on the program. One of the grandest parts of it all was how we all got to choose the win/win solution. We all—teachers, facilitators, and the mayor—chose to play on the same team in support of the children.

The ACE Program in this school and the three others moved forward with plans for the Arab students to begin holding workshops together with their Jewish and Druze ACE counterparts. In total, nearly 400 Israeli students participated that year. Imagine the possibilities!

OUR ENCHANTED PLACE

Our heart is a room without boundaries.

We want to fill it up with love and giving of gentleness, warmth, respect, and understanding.

Our heart is a room full of many pleasant memories. Let's take from there the beautiful moments.

Let's learn from our good experiences and from our mistakes.

Let's learn to forgive, to be forgiving of others, and accept them as they are.

Let's open our hearts to others . . . our heart is full of love.

By Fatan Arin and Hasin Zahar
Girls, ten years old
ACE Student Success Program
Usafia, Israel

Summary

Conflict is often the forerunner to taking corrective action as a return to establishing greater balance or health. Facilitating students—and ourselves—in moving past an *I'm right—You're wrong* position to a willingness to understand another's point of view is essential. Honoring, listening from the heart, and accepting greater responsibility for one's own choices all play a role in resolving conflicts with greater dexterity and mastery.

Exercise For Educators/Parents

Journal

Button Pushing Reflection: *What are your triggers?*

1. Reflect on a situation with a person in your life that triggers you. Describe the situation and the nature of the conflict. Consider how the conflict materializes physically, emotionally, and mentally.

2. Is the conflict with others or is it internal? If it is with others, how might it mirror a conflict you may be experiencing within yourself?

3. How do you typically react when you are in the conflict? Are you reacting out of a need to appear to be right? If so, what are the beliefs associated with that?

After answering these questions, complete the following:

Pause, breathe, and reflect. How might you *respond* rather than *react*? How could you choose to respond effectively and open-mindedly? Envision new ways of approaching this conflict—more responsive and less reactive. Write down your ideas and thoughts.

Explore the mindset of wanting to understand another's point of view. Why might *they* be looking at the situation the way they are? What needs may *they* want to meet? Do I ever have some of those same needs? What might be sitting behind *my* desire to be in the right or to be in control? Are there conflicting beliefs or values of *mine* that are being threatened?

Envision the same situation of conflict, this time with an attitude of response-ability and willingness to take charge of being more effective. What would be different? How would you act or communicate in different ways?

Journal all your responses and any thoughts you have upon completing this reflection.

Exercise For Students/Children

Point of View (from *Making the Best of Me*)

Purpose:

- To promote an awareness of different points of view

- To demonstrate how one's point of view can affect communications

Procedure:

1. Ask students to form groups of four to eight. Instruct them to turn to the young girl/old woman drawing and glance at it briefly, without discussion, and then put their books aside.

2. Ask students to share what they saw in the picture with their group.

3. Have them turn back to the picture and continue their discussion. Assist people who have difficulty identifying both aspects of the drawing.

Discussion:

1. Is there a *correct* way to see the picture? Did you think there was?

2. Is anyone able to see both aspects simultaneously?

3. Name some situations when you knew you were *right* and so did someone else, and both *rights* were different. How did you feel? What happened?

4. How might interpersonal conflicts result from individuals perceiving information differently? How might such conflicts be resolved?

5. What did you feel toward those who saw the drawing the same way you did? Toward those who saw it differently?

6. How does this happen in the world?

7. What strategies can you use in your life to avoid point-of-view conflicts like these?

Chapter Six

Moving From Judgment
to Forgiveness

*Out beyond ideas of wrongdoing and rightdoing there
is a field. I'll meet you there.*

— Rumi

Judging has almost become an art form in our culture. From political pundits on television to social media posts to yard signs, we judge and label each other as being on the right or wrong side, as good or bad. As we discussed in Chapter Five, we seek to be *right*, so we want to control what is labeled *wrong*.

However, we are also judging ourselves. We may judge how we look compared to societal standards. We may see ourselves as not good enough, smart enough, or successful enough. We may declare our way the right way, but often we fail our own expectations.

Internally, we speak these judgments to ourselves, often repeating the hurtful words of others. If our parents told us we were lazy, we may judge ourselves lazy as adults. Then, we tend to speak that same judgment to others, perhaps even calling our own children *lazy*.

We can find ourselves pronouncing silent (or not) judgments, wounding others and ourselves as we walk through our days in a vicious cycle of pain and isolation.

Forgiveness is the doorway to a different viewing point—one of greater acceptance, wisdom, and freedom. As we forgive ourselves for the judgment we have placed against ourselves, we can learn from life's experiences and freely move on. We are then more equipped and available to forgive others.

The hearts of our children often ache from the hurts, hardships, and trauma they keep hidden and secretive. We hope they can nonetheless move through life with a resilient spirit that can overcome the troubles they face. Though we may pray they somehow gather the necessary abilities to maneuver through life's challenges, we know that more needs to be done to provide them with ample tools to draw upon.

It is when hope seems to be gone, and youth feel as if they are alone in a world of confusion and separateness, that the most powerful tools—those of loving and forgiveness—are most needed. These inner skills are more than subjects for inspiring articles; loving and forgiveness are living and teachable qualities of the human spirit that provide youth with strength and hope when all may seem hopeless.

> Forgiveness is the doorway to a different viewing point—one of greater acceptance, wisdom, and freedom.

The Forgiveness Journey

How are we to move kids who are so defensive or lost within their own blight that the common strategies they seek are self-infliction, lashing out and hurting others, retreating, or suicide? In classrooms and youth centers across the country, I have repeatedly witnessed the strength of the human spirit. I have seen youth experiencing a tangible power of loving and forgiveness that has moved them back into affirming life and seeing the brightness of their futures.

The teaching of forgiveness as a life skill needs to occur within a setting where love and forgiveness are alive and practiced. Youth know when the adults around them truly care for them and one another. They can readily see if the adults there genuinely live what they teach. If expressing love, kindness, and consideration for everyone within a school or youth organization is not valued as foundational and is not consciously being developed, then lifting youth into their self-mastery and healing is a long shot. It requires us adults, as authentic role models, taking an honest look at ourselves in the mirror.

In the fall of 2000, inside a rundown multi-purpose room at an under-resourced alternative high school in Kalamazoo, Michigan, a group of sixty students was gathered intimately around an indoor campfire in an activity of sharing what weighed heavy on their hearts. It was the second day of a powerful three-day youth development workshop called ACE. Through their work together on day one, the group had already developed a high degree of trust and safety. As the stories were shared, all were moved to silence and then many to tears. A young man, who had yet to say a word over the first day and a half of the workshop, shared how as a child he witnessed his father killing his mother. A tearful young woman shared how she was raped and the guilt she has carried for being dirty and scarred. Another courageous young man said he'd never met his mother nor his father. He described how, from birth, he had been bounced around from foster home to foster home.

The opportunity to let go of the pain in a room that truly honored and loved them was astounding. In and past their sharing, the students were all soon guided to continue the process of letting go of their pain through the artful practice of forgiveness.

Primary Elements

For loving to develop with a group of young people, some primary elements are needed. These include:

- Dedicated and caring adults

- Adults who are willing to reflect and are committed to their own learning and personal growth

- School, classroom, and home environments where youth are truly respected, honored, listened to, and loved

- Positive environments where youth have a sense of safety and belonging

- Skilled educators who are consciously guiding students in the way of the heart (heartset)

- Established practices by which everyone learns to honor themselves and one another

As the loving and feelings of safety, belonging, and trust are developing, youth can more gracefully embrace learning the art of forgiveness—for oneself and for others. The practice of teaching forgiveness guides youth along a path that leads from tolerance to understanding to compassion.

Teaching forgiveness is grounded in this paradigm: *What if we are all doing the very best we can based on the development of our awareness and consciousness at this point in our lives?* For one to judge another (or oneself) is to consider that we know best what it is they (or we) should be doing. Judgment resides within the world of *right versus wrong and should versus shouldn't.*

Forgiveness, however, is the doorway to a different viewpoint: one of greater acceptance and freedom. As we strive to forgive ourselves for the judgments we have placed, we are able to learn from life's experiences and move on with greater wisdom and freedom. To consider this mindset and heartset requires shifting from a traditional viewing and experiencing of life to seeing through a vastly different window or lens.

> The practice of teaching forgiveness guides youth along a path that leads from tolerance to understanding to compassion.

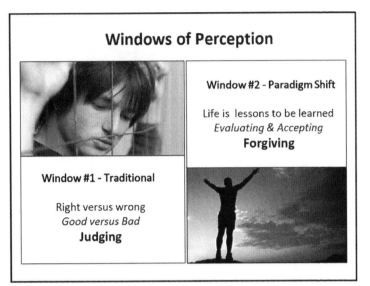

Through the first window, one views life and others through the filter of judgment. Things are right or they're wrong. This is right. This is wrong. This is good. This is bad. We then defend it because this is our belief system. When viewing life through this window, we feel righteous and proper. Life constricts and so does the ability to experience loving and compassion.

The second window sees life through evaluating rather than judgment. Evaluation brings neutrality and objectivity—*this approach works for me or it doesn't*. If it doesn't, rather than reacting and becoming charged with emotion, we work in ways to deal with it. We can choose to look at all experiences as opportunities for growth. *What if I am doing the best that I can in any given moment? If I could have done it better, I would have. Given where my consciousness was in that moment, that was the best that I could do.*

What if the same is true for others? This viewpoint opens the heart. It leads to forgiveness and compassion.

Many teenagers express that the people who have hurt them in the past are not worthy to be forgiven. In my classroom or teen seminars, we discuss how forgiveness is a gift we give *ourselves*. Why? Because we love ourselves and want to be free. It does not mean that we condone or approve of someone's hurtful actions. Malachy McCourt describes it well in noting that "resentment is like eating poison and waiting for the other person to die."[22]

This approach is a startling new way to go through life. We are typically taught to judge, and youth are included in this misdirected teaching. In this radical healing approach, we judge nothing. We can learn from everything and do the best we can in each and every moment.

In EduCare programs, as awareness skills grow, teachers and youth are taught a five-step approach for practicing self-forgiveness:

Step 1 – Be aware of the emotional upset within.

Step 2 – Identify the situation or action that triggered the upset.

Step 3 – Clarify the judgment (of self or others) that you made with yourself.

Step 4 – Reconsider: you are at a choice point; choose to justify the judgment (window #1) or consider compassion/forgiveness (window #2). Forgiveness is a choice we make.

Step 5 – Practice forgiveness: *I forgive myself for judging myself (or others).*

This practice of awareness and then choosing a compassionate way is a life-long practice that youth can learn at an early age and adults can learn at any age! It is beautifully revealed in the following story that a friend shared with me:

A Native American grandfather was talking to his grandson about how he felt. He said, "I feel as if I have two wolves fighting in my heart. One wolf is the vengeful, angry, violent one. The other wolf is the loving, compassionate one."

The grandson asked him, "Which wolf will win the fight in your heart?"

The grandfather answered, "The one I feed."

As adults, we can place the food of judgment, separation, and fear before our young people or provide them with nourishment of loving, forgiveness, and compassion. There are daily, ever-present opportunities to develop forgiveness. The food of loving and forgiveness is the heartiest of nourishment for our children's souls. Forgiveness carries the promise of rippling out and feeding our planet so hungry for deeper understanding, empathy, and compassion.

The Value of Forgiving

> *Forgiveness does not change the past, but it does*
> *enlarge the future.*
>
> — Paul Boose, author

My middle school students and I would sometimes talk about forgiving others. They didn't understand why they should forgive. They would say, "They don't deserve it. It will show my weakness. It will let them off the hook."

But who stays on the hook? We do. The ones who judge. We ingest the poisons of judgment and vindictiveness. When we don't forgive others or ourselves, we stay in an endless loop of judgment and resentment. It limits our perception. It impacts our life. We subject ourselves to carrying around the burden of judgment, which restricts us from taking clear, decisive, and constructive action. It also affects our physical bodies.

Researchers at the University of Tennessee in Knoxville conducted research into the physical effects of forgiveness. They took physical measurements as students were interviewed about hurt and betrayal. While describing their situations, researchers also measured the level of forgiveness demonstrated in these situations. Students who were the most unforgiving had higher blood pressure and tension in their forehead.[23]

Carl Thoresen, director of the Stanford University Forgiveness Research Project, in his book, *Forgiveness: Theory, Research, and Practice*, writes, "We all have the capacity to forgive . . . but [it] takes time because it is the most courageous act one can do."[24]

Often we feel like if we forgive, we're saying that we are condoning or agreeing with the behavior. That isn't what forgiveness means. We simply recognize that forgiveness gives us opportunities to heal, to let go of burdens. Holding on to judgments is like carrying a backpack filled with heavy rocks. If we let go, we lighten the burden we're carrying with each judgment we release. We move forward with greater freedom, with more peace, understanding, and joy.

As with all the *Heartset* skills, it starts with us, with our intention and willingness to forgive ourselves. It is not always easy. We were not taught this. In fact, we were taught the opposite, to beat up on ourselves and to *should* on ourselves continually.

The World of *Shoulds*

In order to move to forgiveness and healing, it is helpful to look at how we set up habits of judgment.

Self-criticism and self-judgment hold back our enthusiasm and our drive. As a classroom teacher, I can remember coming home after a full day with my middle school students, continually listening to my inner critic pick apart the three or four occasions during the day when I thought I had messed up with a student.

My vulture mind was on the loose. *Why didn't I listen to him more when came he came up to me in between classes? I sure screwed up when I lost my temper with that kid who was picking on another student. Boy, was I boring and dull during period three Algebra. No wonder no one was paying attention.*

I would finally think: *Enough already! Mind, please leave me alone.*

All I would think about were the three or four kids or situations where I thought I had royally screwed up. I would not give a moment's notice to the dozens of students I had taught, helped, and listened to. My expectations—my *shoulds*—were off the charts. I sure knew how to *should* on myself.

Forgiveness was my key to helping my mind become my friend. It has been said *if we treated our friends the way we treated ourselves, we wouldn't have many friends.* That saying resonated with me. However, rather than having my mind be that relentless, undermining enemy—my own judge, jury, and executioner, imposing a steady stream of self-inflicted guilty verdicts—I was committed to growing into a clear, directed, and uplifting friend.

Discovering Your *Shoulds*

Take a moment to complete these sentences in your mind or on a piece of paper.

I should...

Others should...

The world should...

Understanding our judgments helps us to better understand how to forgive. Starting with awareness, we can begin to recognize there can be another way—a choice—that says:

- *I understand.*

- *I see myself.*

- *I accept myself.*

- *I see you.*

- *I accept you.*

Judging Yourself and Others

If we didn't gain something from judging, we would not do it. What do you gain from judging? What are your payoffs, or apparent benefits, for judging yourself or others?

Consider if any of these fit for you. When I judge, my payoff is:

- Getting to be right—Have you ever had the most ridiculous discussion that turned into an argument over something petty with someone, even the one closest to you, and you went to the farthest extreme to prove you were right and they were wrong? During the disagreement-turned-argument, you might have forgotten what your reasons or position were. You reached a point where it didn't really matter, as long as you proved you were in the right. We can hold on to wanting to be right so much that we become greatly disturbed and upset.

- Feeling in control or superior—Our drive to be in control has been described as humankind's number one addiction. Sometimes, when we judge, we feel *I am in charge.* In our indignant righteousness—and their wrongness—we can feel as if we have the upper hand (as it should be) and that we are duly handling the situation. And yes, I can remember several relationships where I got to be right and win, and the relationship then fell apart.

- Fuel for self-improvement—I often held the limiting belief that if I judged myself often and harshly enough, it would force me to work harder, get better, and eventually improve myself. My inner critic, my vulture voice, used to tell me: *Be self-critical > work more > achieve more > success.* In actuality, that self-critical voice of self-judgment led me to *Stress more > guilt more > endless negative self-talk more > anxiety, self-hurt, and depression.* There are more effective and healthier strategies for self improvement and motivation than letting the judge rule.

Tips for Self-Forgiving

Increase Awareness

Become more aware of your personal critic. I've called mine my *my vulture voice*. What does yours sound like? When does it appear most frequently? What type of messages does it continually throw at you? Where might you have learned this negative self-talk? From whom?

Have Courage

Face your personal critic and understand your self-judgment in its full force. By noticing it fully, you gain the freedom to step free of it and send it on a long, extended vacation. When it might choose to come knocking on your door again, you can choose again to send it gently on its way one more time. You are not your self-judgments.

Practice Positive Self-Talk

> You are not your self-judgments.

Inside our conversations with ourselves (our self-talk), we create a complicated assortment of ways to doubt and judge ourselves. What if you are not responsible for every thought you now have, but are only responsible for the ones you hold in your mind? The ones you keep ruminating about?

Take Forgiveness Breaks

Take mini forgiveness moments when you notice you are being hard on yourself throughout the day. Say one or more of these forgiveness statements to yourself:

- *I forgive myself for . . .*

- *I forgive myself for judging myself for . . .*

- *I am doing the best I can with what I am dealing with right now.*

- *The truth of the matter is . . .* (add a positive affirmation)

  Example:

  Though I lost my temper for a minute with my students, the truth of the matter is that I am a caring, dedicated, and kind-hearted teacher.

End the day with reflection and forgiveness journaling. You can also do a play-back-the-day visualization at bedtime and insert forgiveness statements for yourself and others.

Summary

After spending over twenty-seven years in prison, Nelson Mandela made this statement about the power of forgiveness:

As I walked out the door toward the gate that would lead to my freedom, I knew if I didn't leave my bitterness and hatred behind, I'd still be in prison.

The move from judgment to forgiveness requires time and patience. A friend of mine once described resentment and judgment as a closed fist. Forgiveness, they said, is releasing one finger at a time until the hand is relaxed. This letting go does not take place in a single moment or even a day. Releasing each finger is process that often involves multiple attempts.

Sometimes, the hand closes into a fist again, they said, but the tension releases more quickly with practice. The good news is that learning to forgive is a *Heartset* skill that we can learn for ourselves and model for our students. It is a gift we give ourselves.

Exercises For Educators/Parents

Journal: My *Shoulds*

Some of these questions may be uncomfortable to address. I invite you to be a courageously uncomfortable and look at some of your *shoulds*, some of your judgments.

Let's start with bringing more awareness to of how we judge ourselves:

1. What do you sometimes judge about yourself?

2. What is the *should* or expectation that you tell yourself?

3. What do you get out of judging? (payoffs)

4. What other choice(s) could you make?

Now try the same reflection in your judgments toward others:

1. Whom do you judge?

2. What do you judge about them?

3. What is the *should* or expectation you have that you or they do not live up to?

4. What do you get out of judging? (payoffs)

5. What other choice(s) could you make?

Now, answer this question: What might sit under your judgments?

The answer may be:

- *I'm afraid.*

- *I've been wronged.*

- *I fear looking weak, foolish, or ignorant.*

- *I am angry or feel slighted.*

- *I am holding on to an upset with another that is unresolved.*

- *I feel misunderstood, and I'm not quite sure how to work my way out it.*

- *I'm not even quite sure what I'm feeling.*

Judging and placing the blame and responsibility on another becomes a simple strategy, an easy resort, a habitual response. We can claim it's their fault. We then give up the freedom of our own personal power of choice by judging. Forgiveness is and always remains an expression of personal power. Forgiveness is the key.

Exercise For Students/Children

Letting Go of Judgment and Guilt: A Journal or Partner-Sharing Activity (from *Making the Best of Me*)

Students can individually journal the following series of questions or verbally answer with a partner.

For example:

1. What do you judge about yourself?

   I judge my intelligence. I think others are smarter than I am. Others get better grades than I do, so I must be stupid.

2. What do you believe "should" be different about yourself?

   I should be smarter and be getting better grades.

3. Is there anything you can do about that?

   I can spend more time studying. I can ask for assistance. I can talk to others and find out how they are getting good grades.

4. How can you let go of the judgment inside yourself?

   I can forgive myself. I can realize that I have done what I have done up until now and acknowledge that I've done the best I knew how at the time. I can accept my best effort and forgive myself for judging myself.

5. How can you be more caring for yourself?

> *I can accept myself the way I am. I can acknowledge myself for ways that I am already expressing my intelligence. I can practice and develop my intelligence more. I can reward myself when I get better grades.*

6. Will you do that? (Be honest)

> *Yes! I am accepting and loving myself!*

Chapter Seven

Turning Challenges
Into Learning Opportunities

It is better to light a candle than to curse the darkness.
— Eleanor Roosevelt

It has been said that we are never given more than we can handle. What if life is constantly giving us opportunities for our learning that are cleverly disguised as *problems?* What if all the challenges we experience—with students, colleagues, strangers, family members, traffic, world conditions—are actually learning opportunities?

By holding a *what-if* attitude and a willingness to look for deeper relevance in whatever comes our way, we open to the likelihood of learning and success. The most challenging issues are perhaps the ones we most need to master.

There is a popular story about a child who woke up on Christmas morning and was surprised to find a heap of horse manure under the tree instead of a collection of presents. Yet, the child was not discouraged. His parents watched him enthusiastically shoveling the manure as he shouted, "With all this manure, there must be a pony in here somewhere!"

Similarly, a recent social media post shares a simple story on turning challenges into opportunities. The person writes:

> Sometimes I just want it to stop. Talk of COVID, protests, looting, brutality. I lose my way. Become convinced that this "new normal" is real life. Then I meet an 87-year-old who talks of living through polio, diphtheria, Vietnam, protests, and yet is still enchanted with life. He seemed surprised when I said that 2020 must be especially challenging for him.

> "No," he said slowly, looking me straight in the eyes. "I learned a long time ago to not see the world through the printed headlines, I see the world through the people that surround me. I see the world with the realization that we love big. Therefore, I just choose to write my own headlines. *Husband loves wife today. Family drops everything to come to Grandma's bedside.* He patted my hand. *Old man makes new friend.*[25]

Seeing Challenges as Our Friends

It's been said that challenges can define us, diminish us, or develop us.

The *Heartset* skill of *Turning Challenges to Opportunities* directly ties in with the *Heartset* skills of *Power of Choice* (attitude) and *Judgment to Forgiveness*. It connects with greater self-care, self-acceptance, and remembering that we are always in a learning process.

Our challenges can be long-standing or show up in the moment. What if we offer a *thank you* to our challenges? This can lead us to a place of gratitude. One expression I heard growing up was: *Well, if you think this is bad, it could be a whole lot worse.*

Michael J. Fox, a veteran actor and author who has lived for decades with Parkinson's disease, understands it well. In addition to coping with his Parkinson's, in 2018 he had surgery to remove a benign tumor wrapped around his spine. As he was learning to walk again, he fell and shattered his left arm. With all that was going on, he was determined to choose a positive attitude. In a 2020 article in *Parade* magazine, Michael shares, "I have Parkinson's and a tumor and a broken arm and I'm still lucky. It could be a lot worse."[26]

The Pandemic of 2020 and Beyond

The coronavirus and our responses to it were a prime example. Looking back, each of us approached the pandemic in many different ways. What opportunities emerged inside of this global challenge, individually and collectively? How did we face these opportunities personally, as communities, a nation, the world? What were our responses? The choices we had were infinite, as were opportunities for growth.

As the pandemic unfolded, organizations, businesses, and non-profits such as EduCare have had to look at their approaches honestly. It was a call for personal and collective leadership. I soon realized that we needed to pivot. We had to move wisely but quickly to take care of ourselves, one another, our nonprofit, and the kids and families we served. We had to look at doing these tasks in new and agile ways.

We needed to pay attention and commit strongly to action. It was an opportunity to reassess how we could better take care of ourselves—how we could support one another with regular check-in calls and fun social times together, even if it had to be through Zoom. How could we be courageous and creative in seeking supplemental funding to keep our programs alive and functioning? How could we find innovative ways to support our kids and families when it came to food, school supplies, and engaging online programming?

Since then, the pandemic has moved our work in serving kids and communities at an accelerated rate, preparing us to strengthen ourselves as a team as we have learned to teach virtually. It propelled us to come together and has made us stronger, more adept, and more proactive. Sponsors, foundations, businesses, and individual donors stepped up to support us in bigger ways than ever. We are still dealing with unexpected twists and turns and are continuing to learn how best to bolster our young people. Through it all, we strive to view the challenges as continual opportunities to develop, serve, and come together.

Within the reality of the never-ending variety of life crises—health issues, loss of loved ones, loss of income, a pandemic—the opportunity and the power of choice to face any challenge is always in our hands. An immediate response might be: *Why bother? It's unfair. It's too hard. I give up.* However, the intention to move with courage to uncover hidden opportunities creates an ability to meet challenges with a spirit of optimism, creativity, and enthusiasm.

M.J. Ryan in her inspiring book, *Attitudes of Gratitude: How to Give and Receive Joy Every Day of Your Life*, mentions Daniel T. Peralta's wise words, "When you were suffering from some difficulty whose blessing is invisible to you, you say the following prayer: *I am willing to see the gift in this experience. May the lessons be revealed to me and may I become stronger and clearer.*"[27]

It has been said: *Never let a good crisis go to waste.* Neil Sprackling, President of US Life and Health Americas, wrote in response to the pandemic: "This is an unprecedented time to examine, to question, and to plant the seeds for accelerated innovation."[28]

The Brooking Institute notes that:

> . . . out of crises can emerge new and incredible opportunities, particularly if traditional approaches and paradigms are questioned and challenged. During a crisis, incentives and motivations change, potentially leading to new cooperative behaviors and even to the creation of new systems or structures. Crises can get the collective adrenaline flowing, focusing minds to solve the problem at hand.[29]

Larry's Story

Thousands have experienced the heavy blow of losing a loved one during the pandemic. Recently my brother's beloved wife, Donna, passed away from COVID.

My brother Larry and I grew up not the best of friends, and it was only in the most recent years that we started to restore our relationship. He is blind, and his wife Donna had been his rock for years. I realized that her illness was an opportunity for me to step up. I always had a deep love for my brother. It was a prayer of mine for years that we grow closer. When I first heard the news that Donna was in the hospital, I quickly took a plane out to be with him in New Jersey.

Larry had also tested positive and was at home, asymptomatic. Over the next days and weeks, we spent much time together in a variety of ways. Our closeness grew through our grieving, reminiscing, consoling, and handling all that needed to be done after Donna's passing and in preparing for his ongoing needs and care. Our connection and love have been wonderfully strengthened through this difficult time.

When his friends were with Larry at the funeral or soon after, he used his grief as an opportunity to lift others. He would pull couples aside, and amongst tears, ask them to make him a promise.

They'd say, "Larry, what promise? Tell me the promise, and I will let you know."

> Grief is to be an opportunity for others to be reminded of the preciousness of expressing love.

He'd reply, "Trust me, just give me a yes or no, and remember that your word is like steel."

Most said yes and Larry then told them, "When you go home and before you go to sleep, hold each other close, give each other a kiss, and share your love for one another."

He knew that his grief was to be an opportunity for others to be reminded of the preciousness of expressing love.

Wisdom: *A Message From White Eagle, Hopi Indigenous*

The moment humanity is going through can now be seen as a portal and as a hole. The decision to fall into the hole or go through the portal is up to you. You were prepared to go through this crisis. Take your toolbox and use all the tools available to you. Learn about resistance of the indigenous and African peoples; we have always been, and continue to be, exterminated. But we still haven't stopped singing, dancing, lighting a fire, and having fun. Don't feel guilty about being happy during this difficult time. You do not help at all being sad and without energy. You help if good things emanate from the Universe now. It is through joy that one resists. Also, when the storm passes, each of you will be very important in the reconstruction of this new world. You need to be well and strong.[30]

Facing Our Challenges: The Four TUDES

In this section, we will talk about *the Four TUDES* we need to face challenges.

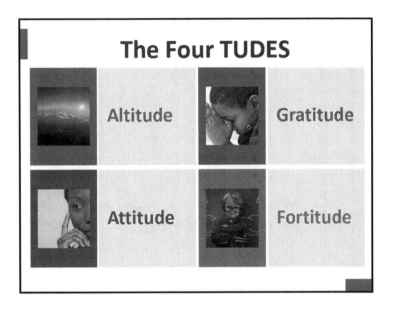

Altitude

Altitude is about elevating our perspective. Am I choosing to view my challenge from an elevated place, a higher altitude? Am I able to stand out from the weeds and look from a different perspective, from a higher perspective, with more objectivity and neutrality?

Rather than being stuck in the mud, can we choose to look at life in new ways through a new lens?

Imagine you're a ranger in the forest, and something threatening is happening. To get a clear assessment of what's going on, you don't want to be down on the ground, surrounded by the trees. You want to be up in the tower, looking out and down over the forest scene with a clear sense of the entire situation rather than being on the ground in the middle of the turmoil, trying to figure out what's going on and where you are most needed.

That higher altitude brings clarity and deeper understanding of what's going on, as well as the causes and potential solutions. This viewing platform of altitude allows the emotional and mental turmoil to calm down, so the information is more clearly gathered, considered, and understood.

How do you gain altitude on your life situations? Rather than just dealing with an onslaught of difficulties and feeling overwhelmed, how do you capture an altitude that's balanced, objective, and effective?

Bringing self-awareness to the moment is a key first step. Realize you are lost and need to step back. Relax and gain greater clarity. Perhaps you need to take a break, go out for a walk, meditate, write, or talk to a trusted friend. You can help yourself by moving back, stepping away, and relaxing.

A helpful common reminder can be *letting go and letting God*, which might translate to *relax and be patient*. Part of shifting to a new altitude might also include action. Part of the letting go may be stepping out from the forest into some fresh air. It may include having the courage to communicate with others more honestly, or in new ways, or to change habitual patterns of behavior that have been at the root of the challenge. Self-awareness is the key, but action—a commitment to a change of behavior—is often also required.

Attitude

> *The mind is its own place, and in itself can make a heaven of Hell, a hell of Heaven.*
>
> — John Milton

Attitude involves becoming aware at all moments that our choices are always with us, no matter what's going on. When we're faced with a challenge and we become aware that we have choices in front of us, what do we take into those moments of choice? Is it a negative attitude or a positive attitude? Do we find joy, happiness, and hopefulness regardless of the situation? We are living in a time when the news shares tremendous stories of insensitivity and injustice. We can also find inspiring examples of great kindness and caring for one another, uplifting stories of people giving and helping out in their communities. While the examples are all around us, the choices are always within us.

One of my most powerful teachers on the TUDE of attitude was a young boy I met at the Fresh Air Fund Camp in New York back in 1968.

> Attitude involves becoming aware at all moments that our choices are always with us, no matter what's going on.

He was a stocky, blond-haired twelve-year-old who had lost both of his legs in a tragic accident. His depression and sadness were evident and, of course, understandable. One warm afternoon, he had decided to go off and sit by himself near his cabin group, who were swimming. I slowly headed over to him and took a seat next to him on the ground.

As I sat quietly next to him, I asked him to look over by the swimming pool. What he saw there were all different special-needs kids swimming. The instructor had no legs, much like the boy next to me. She also had no arms. There she was in the pool, skillfully and joyfully teaching a class of special needs campers how to swim.

I hoped at that moment that something magically would shift inside of him. We talked a bit for a few minutes, and I moved on. Several days later, I noticed him playing in a softball game and enthusiastically using his crutch as a bat. Soon after, he headed off on a trail with other kids for a hike in the woods. Something was starting to shift inside of him. I think it was his commitment to himself and his strength of heart.

It is in our court to always choose a positive attitude regardless of the circumstances or situation. It's not always easy to make that choice, but we have that power. Are we willing to choose a positive attitude to be more effective, to bring more joy into our lives and our relationships, and to look at our challenges as gifts for growing stronger and wiser?

Gratitude

> *The unbearable mark of wisdom is to see the*
> *miraculous in the common.*
> — Ralph Waldo Emerson

To be grateful regardless of circumstances is a magic potion. We can view life as what we have versus what we are lacking.

What cultivates gratitude? Could it be simple things like going outdoors and looking at the beauty of nature, a smile from a family member or friend, or the playfulness of a pet? These small things lift us if we capture and recognize them.

Gratitude is one of the best tools to reframe our mindset as we weather difficult experiences. We can choose to be grateful for learning opportunities, for possible hidden blessings, or for the strength that an especially tough experience provides us. It's impossible to be grateful and worried at the same time.

When I drive, I often shift into gratitude. If I am not feeling at my best as I am leaving the house, I'll start looking at things and take them in: clouds, people, trees, just little things. My self-pep talk is *I'm going to capture moments, people, and things that I'm grateful for today.*

> To be grateful regardless of circumstances is a magic potion.

It's important to nurture gratitude, to spend time in cultivating it. One common practice is creating a gratitude journal and, at the end of the day, taking note of what you're grateful for.

One of my most precious experiences of gratitude was years ago after my wife's last course of treatment for cancer. She was finally on the road to recovery, and she was able to leave the hospital. She could leave her bedroom at home so we could go out for a meal together. As we walked into our favorite neighborhood restaurant and sat down for a breakfast, it struck me how precious this moment was. She was alive and healthy. We were here together, sitting, chatting, and eating after a tough nine-month ordeal. Taking in the fullness that she was alive, and we were able to have this meal once again was precious. My heart was filled with thankfulness, and it still is now.

Fortitude

Fortitude is knowing we have the strength and agency to get through *it*, no matter what. Whatever *it* is, we not only can *survive*—we can *thrive*. We can gain greater confidence and belief in ourselves by choosing to be courageous and having the fortitude to keep moving through challenges. Perseverance and grit become part of our nature. We often learn and become stronger from our most challenging experiences.

Sometimes we must weather it, staying strong, persevering. We have grit. We can endure. Even though it still looks like a challenge, know we are going to move through it.

All four TUDES are in our possession and control. You may not have all four going strong at the same time. They will mix, complement, and elevate one another. You can focus on one, or two, or three of them. *I'm going to bring in gratitude today or I'm just going to weather the storm. I'm not feeling it, but I'm going to go for it regardless.*

People who inspire us the most have often embodied the Four TUDES as part of their moral makeup. Altitude, attitude, gratitude, and fortitude can all blend within us. No matter what the situation is, we can choose the Four TUDES and assist ourselves in turning challenges into learning opportunities.

Summary

Looking at our challenges as a way to learn and grow ultimately strengthens us. As we look back over our lives, we may recognize that our greatest learning often has come as a result of the toughest of times. We can welcome those tough times, as uncomfortable as they are. We then rise above feeling caught or stuck and move to a more objective, balanced, self-caring, and personally effective growth *heartset*.

Exercises For Educators/Parents

Journal

The Four TUDES: Altitude, Attitude, Gratitude, Fortitude

Answer the following questions:

1. What is a challenge you're experiencing at this time?

2. Which TUDE or TUDES can assist you in facing the challenge?

3. What is one step you can take using that TUDE?

Turning Family and Classroom Challenges Into Opportunities for Growth

The next time you find yourself in a power struggle or conflict with your child or student, especially one where you're stuck in a repetition loop, ask yourself these five questions and transform the conflict into growth:

1. What is the challenge or situation?

2. How does the challenge or situation highlight a perceived gap in the child's skills or abilities?

3. What can the child learn from the challenge or situation?

4. What can you learn about yourself through this challenge or situation?

5. How can your relationship with this child deepen as a result of the challenge or situation?

Exercise For Students/Children

Learning From Mistakes

Have your students read the following about mistakes:

One way to approach turning challenges into opportunities is to be willing to learn from making mistakes. Everybody makes mistakes. Mistakes are learning tools that tell you what you need to learn. For instance, if you spell a word incorrectly on a spelling test, the mistake tells you that you need to study the word some more. Thomas Edison made over 1,000 mistakes before he created the light bulb. Good thing he didn't quit. Quitting is what people sometimes choose to do after making a mistake.

When people make mistakes, they often say to themselves: *I'm not perfect, so I must be bad.* What if making mistakes means you're a human being? A mistake is simply an attempt that did not work. That's all. In fact, mistakes can often lead to success through the adjustments you can make to correct them. Some mistakes are more useful than others. Your attitude about your mistakes has a lot to do with their effect on you. What if mistakes are leading you toward learning and success?

1. In your journal, list five mistakes you have made.

2. List what you could learn from each of these mistakes.

   For example:

   I lost my temper with my (brother/sister/friend/parent, etc.) and we had big argument.

   I learned that when I feel that someone embarrasses me, I quickly react and retaliate. I do not have to take their word or opinions about me as truth. I can remember my positive qualities and affirm myself.

Chapter Eight

Giving and Receiving

If you want happiness for an hour, take a nap. If you want happiness for a day, go fishing. If you want happiness for a year, inherit a fortune. If you want happiness for a lifetime, help somebody.

— Chinese Proverb

I learned an unforgettable lesson about giving one day from a little eight-year-old girl carrying a bag of canned foods. The day before, she and others in her fifth grade class at a public school in one of the most economically deprived neighborhoods in South L.A. had prepared boxes of sack lunches to take with them on a class field trip to feed the homeless.

As the students were stepping onto the school bus that morning for their class trip, I clearly remember her laboring with a heavy grocery bag full of canned goods.

"Why did you bring all this food?" I asked her.

She answered that her mom wanted to make sure she had plenty to give to the hungry people she would meet at the beach that day. *They should have enough food*, she had said. Her mom's simple expression of generosity from a family that likely was just getting by themselves touched my heart. How inspiring that this young girl of limited means was learning such a profound lesson of overflowing kindness and humanity.

Giving and Receiving

You receive through the same channel you give through. If you give through a tiny, almost-closed opening, that is the same opening you receive through, and the love will come back to you all closed up. But if you are loving openly and unafraid, not caring whether someone else loves you in return, you have 100 percent of the love.

— John-Roger, educator and author

As we give freely without thought of return, we expand in unforeseen and miraculous ways. The joy of giving is its own reward. The *gift of giving* grows as we keep love around by letting it go. In unconditionally giving, the compassionate heart expands, and its warmth radiates and heals both the giver and the receiver. The most special days for my students each year were our trips to nursing homes, food banks, and homeless shelters where they got to experience, through their acts of service, delightful satisfaction and unadorned joy.

> In unconditionally giving, the compassionate heart expands, and its warmth radiates and heals both the giver and the receiver.

As there are enormous personal rewards in the giving, there is also an important need to be on the receiving end. The reward from giving and the benefit of receiving go hand in hand. When we welcomingly receive, we are providing others with the gratifying opportunities for them to give. We also get to fill our own cup so that we are more equipped and ready to give of our overflow.

For years, receiving openly and gracefully had not been one of my strong suits. When our son Jeff was in preschool, he returned home one day and came prancing in with a crafts project he had created especially for me. I took his gift in a quick and perfunctory way and went right back to my work. His face dropped, and I realized immediately this exchange, which could have been so special, was an instant heartbreak.

My flashing red alert of guilt then went off. *Stu, you need to slow down and see what is going on here. This is a precious moment that you are about to bulldoze through. By simply receiving, here is a precious opportunity to esteem your son whom you deeply love.* Receiving is a gift of honoring another. I needed to open up myself to receive these ever-present precious moments that were being offered to me continually in my life. As a line in one of my favorite songs says: *Take the time to live, all that your life has to give.*

It was a lesson that took root in me. I knew I wanted to, and could, do better. I am the one who loves to give to others, but I could start breathing more fully, relaxing more, and becoming more aware of what was being presented to me—moment by moment. I could take a mindful pause and always choose to receive fully as well as look to give generously.

Do you find it easier to give than receive? For many people, that's the case. Or are you more comfortable receiving than giving? Would you say you're about equal? How do we activate the giving and the receiving? When they come together, there's a flow of energy that's amazing. Inner contentment and life fulfilment come from expanding both our giving and receiving.

The *Heartset* skill of giving and receiving is the capstone of all our eight *Heartset* skills. The previous seven *Heartset* skills build upon each other and splendidly tie together in the skillset of giving and receiving.

By giving, we receive, and by receiving, we give. In giving, we receive the benefits of greater kindness, health, and happiness because our compassion comes back around. Our receiving is splendidly intertwined with our giving. It's easy to forget that receiving is also a gift of giving. We give another the chance to be compassionate and gracious. We provide them with the gratifying opportunity to be a giver.

What if our world only had givers, and there was no one receiving? We givers would be out of business. In receiving, we expand our ability to source and absorb the wisdom and valuable support from others. We experience the mosaic of our interdependence and rich connection.

This wonderful weave of giving and receiving is expressed by Jacqueline DeGroot in her article "Jewish Philanthropy: The Concept of Tzedakah." She writes, "In Hebrew, the word meaning 'to give' is *Natan*. In Hebrew and in English, the word can be read forward and backward, so when we think about philanthropy and the idea of *to give* it is also about *to receive*."[31]

We give and receive not only material items. We may give and receive information, support, wisdom, encouragement, empathy, understanding, and love. As we freely share ideas, abilities, and caring, our learning multiplies. It can be as simple as giving someone the gifts of your time or attention. One of the greatest gifts we can give is letting someone share what's going on with them.

Two Directions

The art of giving and receiving is a fulfilling life-long practice. Both giving and receiving have two directions. The most obviously giving direction is to give outwardly to others. But one that you may forget is to give inwardly to yourself. When you first take care of yourself, you will be more equipped to give to others. This self-care ideal becomes the foreground for the *Heartset* skills of self-honoring, praising, and empathetic listening.

Similar to giving, receiving has two primary directions or sources: receiving from others and—the one often less practiced—receiving from ourselves. Consider being not just mindful of listening to others but also mindful of listening to yourself—your feelings, your needs, and your intuition. This gift of providing yourself with the time to develop and receive deeper wisdom from inside can be life changing.

Other practices for receiving from ourselves include:

- Self-acknowledging and self-forgiving

- Reflective insight and self-support

- Providing ourselves with play and fun

When we are giving less to ourselves, we are sometimes stirred by receiving generosity from family and friends. When I am being the most hard on myself, I am reminded of the beauty of light-hearted and humorous moments with fun-loving friends who draw me out of my serious mindedness. These are wonderful *joy triggers*: choosing to do things to spark joy as a way to lift or nurture ourselves. Joy triggers come in many different forms—dancing, painting, walking in nature, singing, playing music, calling or visiting a friend, or sharing a joke or an amusing story.

Receiving from others can be difficult as it requires courage and openness. When my wife and I were first dating, I would come home from work stressed out and sit on the couch grimacing and grunting as I tried to reach back and massage my shoulders.

Candace would say, "Are you asking for something you haven't said out loud?"

Sheepishly, I would reply, "Would you mind rubbing my shoulders?"

"Sure, and it'd be easier if you just told me. I wouldn't have to read your body language all the time."

In the boldness of knowing we're worthy to receive, sometimes we have to be courageous enough to ask for what we want. Asking is an essential part of the formula. Asking for what you want may mean overcoming a lack of self-worth or the fear of rejection (*What if they say no?*) or an assortment of limiting beliefs about asking others for support or assistance.

The willingness to ask creates a freedom in the flow of giving and receiving and the ever-expanding experience of human kindness and heartfelt connection. Opening that portal requires recognizing the multitude of choices in our mindset and our inner beliefs about giving and receiving.

Giving From Lack

Giving and receiving can be sourced within ourselves from a place of lack, underflow, or deficit or from a place of fullness, overflow, enthusiasm, or gratefulness.

When giving is coming from a feeling of lack, underflow, or deficit, it is often expressed in one of the following ways:

- *Giving to get*

  This kind of giving is transactional in nature. If I give to you, I'm expecting that I'll get something back in return. If I don't receive something in return, I am justified in feeling disappointed, betrayed, or let down. *Look at all that I've given, and they have not matched up in return.*

- *Obligation, repayment, and keeping score*

  Once I have been given to, I'm now obligated to give back. I feel I should or need to reciprocate. It is tit for tat.

- *Ego identity*

  When I give, I can pat myself on the back for being a good and kind person.

- *Recognition*

  I am giving out of a desire to be noticed for being generous. *Look at me and see how much I do for others.*

- *Power*

  Giving places me in a position where others are indebted to me.

Many of us have been raised with limiting belief systems that equate our self-worth with the degree we give to others. You may feel as if you always need to be in giving, contributing, and caretaking roles and believe that the more you give, the more worthwhile you are as a person. This impulsive, unconscious need to constantly give grows into a hard-driving taskmaster. The act of giving then becomes a duty, an obligation or a *should* that easily depletes us. We then feel guilty when we don't give enough of our time and attention to a person or cause.

Our giving needs to include ourselves so we can replenish. If not, we can easily feel exhausted, resentful, or even bitter as we give. Giving from lack, underflow, or deficit produces overwhelm, judgment, anxiety, and disappointment. It closes the door on the flow and expansion of health and happiness.

Giving From Fullness

Then there's giving from fullness, overflow, joy, and thankfulness. The inner dialogue, beliefs, and qualities in this type of giving include:

- *I have plenty, more than I need.*

- *I give with the natural joy of giving.*

- *I take excellent care of myself by giving to myself first. I then have more than enough to share with others.*

- *I give with no strings attached. Rather than keeping score, I am a joyful giver, reaping the benefits of my unconditional giving.*

- *Giving comes back to me multiplied in unexpected and miraculous ways.*

In order to give to others in healthy ways, we need to continually remember to give first to ourselves. Only then can we give from the overflow. We take care of ourselves so we can take care of each other.

As Dr. Mario Martinez explains, "A benign boundary is reached when you can calibrate between resentment (you did too much) and guilt (you did not do enough). This leads you to take care of yourself without ignoring the needs of others."[32] The Tibetan Buddhists call this *inclusive compassion* as you include yourself in the compassionate act.

To give from fullness requires practicing good self-care in many different ways:

- Physically (sleep, rest, breathing, exercise, nutrition)

- Emotionally (self-forgiveness, joy triggers, time with friends, acts of kindness)

- Mentally (positive self-talk, growth mindset, gratitude, journaling)

- Spiritually (meditation, reflection, prayer)

Types of Giving

Giving from underflow / deficit
- Give to get, keep score, repayment
- Obligation or should
- Desire for recognition

Giving from overflow / surplus
- I have plenty, more than I need
- Unconditional, no strings attached
- With the joy of giving

As we take good care of ourselves and fill our own cup, giving becomes an expression or act of compassionate service. We can give of the natural overflow. Acts of service to others, it has been said, are the highest form of loving. It is the nature of the unconditionally loving heart to give. The joy of giving is a wonderful gift we give ourselves.

> *Everybody can be great because anybody can serve.*
> *You don't have to have a college degree to serve.*
> *You don't have to make your subject and verb agree*
> *to serve. You only need a heart full of grace, a soul*
> *generated by love.*
> — Martin Luther King, Jr.

The Art of Receiving

Receiving acknowledges and honors the goodness and intrinsic value of the giver.

I learned a powerful lesson in the art of giving and receiving at a 7-Eleven store. Late one night as I got out of my car to pick up a snack, a man who looked like he was homeless approached with towels and a water bottle in hand. He asked me if I wanted to have my windows washed. My first thought was no. Then I thought *what the heck* and nodded okay. As I walked inside and bought myself a sandwich, I looked out the window toward the parking lot just a few feet away. I stopped in my tracks. With amazing diligence, this man was impeccably cleaning all parts of my car's windshield, paying ever so close attention to the tiniest of smudges. I was enamored by how exquisitely he went at it. I was so taken by the extent of his giving that I felt as if I was watching much more than a man simply washing a car window. He was polishing a prized jewel that just happened to be my car windshield.

> Receiving acknowledges and honors the goodness and intrinsic value of the giver.

As I walked outside, he seemed not to notice me and just kept on going. It was obviously much greater than just a chore to him; it was his opportunity to deeply serve. I did not want to stop this sacred scene as I was riveted by the awesomeness of his giving. He soon stopped as if he felt done and looked at me. I briefly thanked him, gave him a generous tip, and watched him turn and go inside the store. He had gifted me much more than the money I had given him. Here was an ordinary man with an extraordinary capacity to give and serve wholeheartedly. My gift to myself was to experience his remarkable gift of unconditional giving. The splendid reward he received was the one he had given himself—the fullness of his giving.

Receiving From Lack

Sometimes people are challenged in receiving because they believe they do not deserve to receive. They believe they haven't done enough, are not worthy enough, are not good enough. When good news comes their way, people give them a compliment, or something miraculous happens, they deny, filter, or deflect it by thinking *Why me? I don't deserve it.*

When we allow ourselves to dwell in negative, self-demeaning, or *stinking thinking,* we build limiting belief systems that unwittingly hold us back from receiving. We may carry unconscious belief systems about what's right and wrong in terms of giving and receiving. Each mind has cascading limiting thoughts. It's not what we think in our minds that is critical; it is what we hold or keep ruminating on in our minds that is essential. Limiting beliefs are strengthened when we give special credence or authority to the comings and goings of our negative thoughts.

We could choose to think: *It's just another thought. So what? Just because I think it, doesn't make it necessarily true.* When we put enough focus and attention on our negative beliefs, we empower them. The key is not positive thinking, which is impossible to maintain; the key is choosing a positive focus. The choice of maintaining a positive focus replaces the dilemma of struggling to maintain consistent positive thinking. We are all going to experience an ongoing assortment of negative thoughts. That's just the way our minds operate.

However, we don't have to hold a negative focus. The more we become aware of our limiting mental beliefs, the more we can kindly think: *Thank you, but I don't choose to live in that limiting belief. The truth of the matter is I am worthy and deserving of being in the abundant flow of giving and receiving*. We are capable of this refocusing when our minds wander; we can redirect ourselves to a positive and affirming set of beliefs.

Just as there are barriers we place within ourselves that limit the extent of our giving, we also set limitations on how we receive. When receiving is sourced or is coming from a feeling of lack, underflow, or deficit, it is expressed as:

- *Begrudgingness*

  This response comes from feeling as if I really don't want to receive but that I should. *I better take this gift because if I don't, they'll think worse of me or that I'm not a gracious receiver.*

- *Obligation, repayment, and keeping score*

  These situations result from believing that the giver doesn't really want to give me something. Maybe they feel like they must pay me back for something I did in the past. It is not because they really want to give it to me now. I am now going to be obligated to give them something in return.

- *Unworthy to receive*

  I don't believe I truly deserve gifts.

- *Mistrustful*

  I don't trust the giver because I believe they're in it for something. *I wonder what they are after.* I push or hold them back because I think they have an agenda. This may at times be true, but sometimes, we may be quick to prejudge their intentions.

A Story: Receiving From Fullness, Openness, and Gratefulness

Why was Tom, a close friend, handing me an envelope with $500? When he stepped into my house that day, I was in the depths of depression. I was devastated by my wife's recent cancer diagnosis. I was at a low point in generating income, and I knew the medical costs would be tough. I felt overwhelmed, not knowing how I would be able to take care of Candy and our then five-year-old son Jeff, who was entering first grade.

It all seemed insurmountable. In small ways, I leaked word out to a few friends that we needed help. The flood of assistance was unbelievable. Friends collected money, provided food, and made sure our son was taken care of. One dear friend came to live with us to help with Jeff and our household needs. My colleagues pulled together and wonderfully covered my workload. Neighborhood friends took our son in for dinner and weekend overnights and made sure his friendship circle remained strong. My closest friends guided me in taking care of myself as well. My heart flooded with gratitude, over and over. This perpetual giver—me—was learning the importance and necessity of receiving in big doses.

Some of the key elements of mastering the art of expanded receiving are:

- *Worthiness*—I believe I am worthy to receive, just as I am deserving of happiness and success.

- *Gratefulness*—I am a grateful receiver and am thankful for great good that comes to be in my life.

- *Honoring another*—As I receive, I acknowledge the generosity and goodness of others.

Types of Receiving

Receiving from...
- Should
- Reluctant
- Repaying

Receiving from...
- Worthiness
- Gratefulness
- As an act of honoring another

For many years, I realized EduCare's success was closely related to the degree of my worthiness and the value that I as president and others held for EduCare. The more we appreciated and honored the beautiful work we were doing, the more we seemed to receive greater support, donations, unexpected resources, contracts, and an influx of terrific staff and volunteers.

Alongside the self-worth was an increasing level of gratitude. We were so grateful for all the support that EduCare had been given and the opportunities we had to assist so many young people and their families. This combination of worthiness, reaching out, asking for support or assistance, and gratefulness seem to catalyze EduCare's good fortune.

At this point in our discussion, I invite to you pause and turn to the Journal Exercises at the end of the chapter and complete the exercise on limiting beliefs.

As you practice reframing your limiting beliefs into positive, constructive, affirming statements, giving can become contagious. There are many stories of people paying it forward, paying for the next person in line at a fast-food takeout drive-through or at a tollbooth, paying for the car behind them. When limiting beliefs are replaced with positive and affirming beliefs, giving ignites more giving, and a virus of kindness can erupt.

A Story: The Gift of Giving

The group of partnering high school teachers was adamantly opposed to their classes of low-achieving black students visiting a nearby nursing home. They feared their students would be out of hand and would leave a negative mark on the school's reputation. They eventually acquiesced, and off we bused to a local residential facility that housed mainly Italian American seniors. They were the only senior's home that agreed to allow our EduCare program students in.

The students were nervous as they slowly began to visit the rooms and engage in conversations and gift exchanges with the residents. We had Polaroid cameras to take wonderful close-ups they could give the seniors. We joined in the activity room for singing and bingo games and before long, there it was—happiness, fun, smiles, and laughter. By the time we needed to leave at the end of the day to get back to school, kid after kid did not want to go home. They would tell me, "No, this is my new grandmother. I can't leave her right now." We assured them that we would help them create opportunities in the future to return soon.

The Science of Giving

Giving enhances us on so many levels. It makes us feel happy, making our lives richer and healthier in many ways. Jason Marsh and Jill Suttie write that giving ". . . activates regions of the brain associated with pleasure, social connection, and trust, creating a 'warm glow' effect."[33] The brain's pleasure circuits that make us feel good and regulate emotional responses are activated by giving. Similar to people who run and get a *runner's high*, you're motivated to give more. Instead of reaching for a piece of chocolate cake when we are down, we can get a boost from doing something to benefit someone else.

A group of my friends and I knew this intuitively back in college. On a vacation road trip, in a car full of close friends, Barbara would sometimes get depressed and sad and reach for her bag full of candy. We thought of something different. Whenever she would drop into despair and go for her candy, we would stop the car, jump out, circle around her, and give her a big group hug. Then we'd jump back in the car and continue on our way. The result? Less depression. Fewer calories. Happy Barbara. Happy us, the givers.

Giving is good for our health. A wide range of research has linked different forms of generosity to better health, even among the sick and elderly. Giving promotes cooperation and social connections. When we give to others, we also feel closer to them. "Being kind and generous leads you to perceive others more positively and more charitably," writes Sonja Lyubomirsky in her book *The How of Happiness*, and this "fosters a heightened sense of interdependence and cooperation in your social community."[34]

We get a neurological rush when we give. Per Dr. Beth McQuiston, a board-certified neurologist and medical director at Abbot, multiple scientific studies show that volunteering "helps decrease stress, cortisol levels (which can raise blood sugar levels and deplete the immune system) and lower blood sugar."[35] She mentions the so-called *helpers' high* that National Institutes of Health neuroscientist Jorge Moll studied that leads to a release of addictive feel-good neurotransmitters like oxytocin and vasopressin. McQuinston comments, ". . . they get a high from it, just like running, love, money, and sex can do. But for most people, giving just makes you feel good."[36]

Summary

Giving and receiving love is vital to human existence. It is the glue that binds families, friends, communities, cultures, and nations. And as you begin to share the *Heartset* skills with yourself and others, you are part of that glue, that connector binding our world with more love, more heart, and more caring.

Exercises For Educators/Parents

Journal: *Limiting Beliefs on Giving and Receiving*

This exercise is an opportunity to explore your *limiting beliefs* as a way to move past them into an expanding cycle of giving and receiving. Spend about 5–10 minutes writing out whatever comes to mind regarding your limiting beliefs on giving and receiving.

1. *If I give, then . . .*

   Examples of limiting beliefs:

   I am selfish and there will be less for other people.

   There won't be enough left over for me.

   People won't appreciate it. They won't like it anyway. It won't be the right thing to give.

   I will need to give continually to show how much I care.

   It will become expected and then I'll be taken advantage of.

   I will never be able to give enough. I will fall short of what is needed or expected so why give at all.

2. *If I receive, then . . .*

   Examples of limiting beliefs:

   I will be indebted to pay them back in return.

   They will have power or control over me.

I feel guilty because it's selfish to receive.

Others are going to expect something back from me.

It means I'm not strong and powerful on my own; I'm needy. And I don't want to be needy. I will feel vulnerable.

I have to find a way to reciprocate and that's a lot of work.

3. Practice contesting these limiting beliefs and then reframing or replacing them with positive, affirming statements or beliefs. See examples below.

Limiting belief: *If I give, there won't be enough left over for me.*

Affirming belief: *As I give, abundance comes to me in perfect ways for the highest good of all.*

Limiting belief: *If I receive, I'm not strong or powerful on my own. I am needy.*

Affirming belief: *It is smart and resourceful to ask and receive support. Highly successful people lean on others and receive assistance.*

Exercises For Students/Children

Make My Day (from *Making the Best of Me*)

There are many ways to brighten up your own and other people's day. Some ideas are:

1. Write a letter or short note to someone special in your life (grandparents, brother, sister, friend, teacher) and let them know how much you appreciate them, the things you have learned from them, and how much you care. Then mail it. Write one also to yourself.

2. Today, spend at least five minutes in front of the mirror using positive self-talk out loud as you look into your eyes.

3. Today, call or write someone you care about and tell them how grateful you are for their presence in your life.

4. Call someone you admire and look up to. Invite them to lunch and take time to talk and share with them about the qualities in them you admire.

5. Today, compliment or verbally appreciate at least three people.

6. Today, as you go through the day, tell yourself at least three positive compliments.

Add some of your own ideas and choose to practice one or more.

Making a Difference: Service (from *Making the Best of Me*)

Purpose:

- To enhance awareness of each individual's power to make a difference

- To build group cohesiveness

Procedure:

1. Discuss the concept of service. Define it. Discuss unconditional giving: giving to give, not to get something back in return; giving from the heart or caring; and it is the thought and feeling behind the gift that counts, not the size.

2. Explore whether students feel they can make a difference in the world around them. Why or why not? Assist students in finding ways in which they already are serving their family, friends, school, and/or community without even knowing it.

3. Have students complete the activity questions.

4. In small groups, or as a large group, share world visions. You may want to create a mural depicting the group's world visions, Discuss similarities/differences. Brainstorm ways to bring the world closer to that vision.

5. In small groups, or as a large group, decide on a way to serve the school or community. Make a plan, assign tasks, arrange for materials, and do it.

Activity Questions:

1. *I can make a difference in my family by . . .*

2. *I can make a difference in my school by . . .*

3. *I can make a difference in my community by . . .*

4. *What is the best you can imagine for the world?*

5. *One thing I could do this week to bring the world closer to my vision is . . .*

6. *Are you willing to do that? Be honest.*

7. *Who could assist you?*

Exercises For Educators, Parents, Students, And Children

Journal on Giving and Receiving: Part 1

Answer the following questions in your journal:

1. What would I like to give? (to myself and to others)

   Example: *One thing I'd like to give to myself is more personal time to go outdoors and enjoy the weather and the beauty of nature. What I'd like to give to others is more patience. I'm finding that when I get a little stressed, I can be tense and impatient.*

2. What would I like to receive? (from myself and from others)

   Examples: *I'd like to receive more acceptance from myself when I experience mood shifts during challenging times. I'm going to be impatient, I'm going to be sad, and I'm going to be tired. I'd like to receive more understanding and acceptance as my shifts seem to be more pronounced now.*

   What I'd like to receive from others is more patience for me. When I am out of sorts, impatient with someone, and then apologize, I would like them to be more understanding and forgiving of me.

3. What can I do differently in order to open to greater giving and receiving?

Example: *What I can do differently is to breathe more deeply, to pause more regularly, and to trust that each situation will be resolved. I don't have to be the master fixer for everything. It may be past my abilities. I can have more faith and understanding.*

4. What might be the result of opening to greater giving and receiving?

Example: *I would be more relaxed, joyful, and happy with myself and with others. My relationships with others would be more honest, authentic, empathetic, and supportive.*

Journal on Giving and Receiving: Part 2

Answer these questions from your own experience:

1. Describe a time when you felt wonderful about giving. What is it you gave, and what did you receive in the giving?

2. Describe a time when you were open to receive. What is it you received? How did you feel? What might you have given by receiving?

Conclusion

This book has been built upon the dream of putting love into action. A dream of sharing my ongoing life lessons for enriching a way of being, a way of living, learning, and teaching sourced from the richness of the *Heartset* skills.

I invite you to please imagine with me the future of education and our society, where love is the foundation of educating our children. A future where all of our young people are deeply seen, heard, known, and valued.

Imagine classrooms and schools where human connection and kindness is the norm, where no child would go unnoticed, where students who may want to remain invisible and are in danger of slipping through the cracks are seen, not forgotten, and are treasured and loved.

Imagine a school, an educational system, a government, and a society that steps up like a family, a deeply caring family.

Imagine people looking with eyes willing to see each other, not focusing on differences that we think divide us but on the goodness of who we each truly are.

I hope this book inspires each of us to practice more loving wherever we are and with each person we are with—including ourselves. My sincere thanks to you as together we bring forward a world filled with greater kindness and compassion.

Next Steps

I warmly invite you to contact me at stu@educarefoundation. com to explore ways to bring *Heartset® Education* to your school and community. EduCare provides diverse offerings of in-person and virtual programs, trainings, and curriculum, with services for students, teachers, and parents. For more information, please contact info@educarefoundation.com or visit our website at educarefoundation.com.

Also, *Heartset® Education's* precursor, *Making the Best of Me: A Handbook for Student Excellence and Self-Esteem*, authored by Sindy Wilkinson and me, is a comprehensive collection of practical, enjoyable social-emotional learning activities based on our many years of classroom experience. Written for use by teachers, counselors, and youth group leaders, this valuable handbook includes an introduction to the adult's role in building self-esteem. Chapters and interactive exercises cover the topics of self-esteem, teambuilding, communication skills, personal responsibility, achieving excellence, reaching out to one's family and community, and personal journal writing. *Making the Best of Me: A Handbook for Student Excellence and Self-Esteem* is also available on Amazon and is an excellent companion book to *Heartset Education: A Way of Living and Learning*.

Acknowledgments

Experiencing and expressing gratitude is at the center of developing a growth *Heartset*. I thank the multitudes of students and young people who have touched my life, made me laugh, inspired, and brought out the best of me. I thank the many caring teachers and educators who provided me with a picture of what the field of education could be.

I thank my beloved wife Candace for her loving presence, comfort, and encouragement through the years, and our son Jeffrey for his light-hearted joy and kindness.

I acknowledge my spiritual teachers, John-Roger and John Morton for their inspiring examples of loving service. You helped me open my eyes and my heart to who I am.

Special thanks to Russell Bishop, co-creator of Insight Seminars, and Drs. Ron and Mary Hulnick, co-directors of the University of Santa Monica, who years ago graciously allowed me to adapt many key principles taught in their transformational seminars and classes for EduCare's work in schools.

I thank my mentors, teachers, and colleagues in the field of spiritual psychology and transformational education—especially Pat Peake, Michael Funk, Parker Palmer, David Allen, Jack Canfield, Jose Navarro, Mark Samuel, Greg Stebbins, Nick Segal, Father Gregory Boyle, Tom Boyer, Leslie Boyer, Terry Tillman, Robert Razz, David Raynr, Diane Botticelli, Patti Rayner, Wayne Pepper, Mike Connor,

Rachael Jayne, Mary Ann Somerville, and the many incredible facilitators and friends at Insight Seminars.

My heartfelt thanks to my dedicated colleagues, staff, and board members at EduCare Foundation, who collectively have been devoted to the vision of a world where young people are loved and empowered—especially Jill Jacobson, Katherine Hall, Armando Diaz, Lorena Sanchez, Robert Underhill, Leah Jean, Lynn Farwell, Holly Engelman, Janvie Cason, Frank Vitale, Eliana Farias, LaNell Williams, Bryn Drescher, Margalit Ward, Yesenia Leon, George Hernandez, Raul Fernandez, Jennie Rosenbaum, Nicholas Brown, Susan Saltz, Joey Hubbard, Tom Forbath, Kamin Samuel, Brian Evans, Jolie Martin, Peter Felsmann, Victoria Coulter-Bloch, and Eldrick Bone.

I acknowledge the incredible EduCare Program Managers— Gerardo Mungaray, Jeanaah Sampson, Daniel Cortes, Manuel Pool, Gigi Barba, Coila Romero, Rocio Rodriguez, Joseph Montesdeoca, Sandra de Tovar, and the dozens of our EduCare coordinators and ACE Initiative Administrators who make EduCare's work of lifting our students possible each and every day.

I acknowledge the committed individuals and educational leaders I have had the privilege to team up with: Jose Navarro, Esther Jantzen, Margaret Peake, Barbara Knight-Meyers and Tom Meyers, Scott and Janet Ringer, Leigh Taylor-Young Morton, David and Amy Bransky, Sindy Wilkinson, Genie Ford, Steve and Karla Chopyak, Matthew and Marilyn Molitch, Eric and Elyssa Nelson, Richard Powell, Kelly Raleigh, Ofer Weismann, Inbal Gelfarb, Aviva Tal, Rinaldo and Maritza Porcile, Patrick Belisle, Siouxsie Koch, Michelle Perrenoud, Jeff Davis, Frank Escobar, Al Cortes, Harry Talbot, Peter Bort, Mary Jo Ginty, Pedro Noguera, Sam Piha, Tia Quinn, and multitudes of others.

I thank my brother, Larry Semigran, for being a role model of positive attitude, grit, and humor, for having my back when we were growing up, and for demonstrating incredible courage in the face of enormous challenges.

I thank my dear friends whose joy, love, and support help make the journey fun.

Thanks to Keith and Maura Leon at Babypie Publishing for their guidance and encouragement and to delightful Karen Burton, my talented editor, for her honest and clear coaching throughout the writing process. Thanks also to Hillary Neumeister, John Cawley, and Laren Bright for their feedback and support with my writing.

I share my appreciation of all the many charitable foundations, organizations, individual donors, and supporters of EduCare since 1990 for their steadfast belief in the value of heart-centered education.

I am forever grateful to my mom and dad, whom I love and carry in my heart as steadfast role models of *Heartset* in action. I thank you.

I thank all those whom I have had the privilege to study and teach with over the years—for touching my heart and inspiring me to keep giving and serving.

I thank God for the joy and privilege to be blessed with my life and all that continually unfolds in my experiencing and sharing greater loving.

About EduCare Foundation

EduCare provides compassionate learning environments of genuine caring, self-discovery, and empowerment, helping young people to flourish in spite of life's challenges.

Heartset® Education, EduCare's unique platform for social-emotional learning (SEL), helps youth flourish and realize their full potential by addressing these needs. It promotes and teaches self-awareness, personal responsibility, empathy, and compassion in the face of life's uncertainties and challenges.

Heartset for Students

Currently serving over 30,000 students annually, EduCare offers programs (virtually and in-person) incorporating proven social-emotional learning principles empowering students to thrive.

- **ACE: (Achievement and Commitment to Excellence) Program** is EduCare's flagship student program. Firmly rooted in social-emotional learning, ACE promotes the skills and self-confidence needed to achieve academic excellence.

- **ACE Initiative (AI) Schools** weaves *Heartset Education* into the fabric and culture of a school throughout the year, supporting students, teachers, and parents to build schools infused with kindness, empathy, and human connection.

- **ACE Heartbeats** (*Virtual Heartset Social-Emotional Learning Workshops*) are a by-product of the ACE youth development program. These highly interactive workshops focus on **success, positive school climate** and **connection,** and **character-building skills.**

- **Afterschool Programs** provided within the framework of *Heartset Education* go beyond simply providing a safe afterschool environment and actively engage students in life-changing opportunities for learning, leadership, and growth.

- **Specialized Student Services** include Case Management Support, English Language Learners Support, Substance Abuse Prevention and Intervention, and Leadership and Service Learning.

Heartset **for Educators** addresses the many challenges faced by teachers, school staff, and school administrators. These programs assist in shifting the culture of learning, inspiring schools to create communities of caring that address both student and educator needs. Teachers learn to establish successful learning environments infused with caring, connection, and proven SEL practices.

Heartset **for Parents** recognizes that youth development starts at home. EduCare provides Parent and Family Skills Development Workshops that teach strategies for creating a nurturing home environment and building a strong foundation to support children's academic and personal growth.

The EduCare Foundation is a 501(c)3 nonprofit organization, and all donations are tax-deductible as allowed by law. Federal Tax ID: 95-428-5350.

For more information and to learn more about EduCare Foundation, contact info@educarefoundation.com or stu@educarefoundation.com.

About The Author

Stu Semigran has more than forty years' experience as an educator, teaching in urban public schools and subsequently developing and facilitating training programs for youth and adults in educational settings worldwide. As co-founder and president of the EduCare Foundation, Stu has trained thousands of professionals, youths, educators, and parents in leadership development, afterschool and expanded learning programs, and social-emotional learning.

Since 1990, EduCare has served over 300,000 students and 45,000 teachers and parents across more than 450 schools. Currently, EduCare is the largest provider of high school afterschool programs within the Los Angeles Unified School District. Stu has developed innovative social-emotional development curricula, including *Making the Best of Me: A Handbook for Student Excellence and Self-Esteem*, which is used in schools worldwide. He initiated EduCare's *Heartset® Education* model that guides educators in building kinder and more compassionate classrooms and schools.

A highly skilled and motivating speaker with an exceptional rapport with people of all ages, Stu has appeared on radio and television, and has presented at conferences internationally. Stu's kind-hearted and innovative leadership is widely noted. Stu recently served on the CA Department of Education's Social and Emotional Learning (SEL) State Workgroup. In 2012, he was recognized as a David Chow Foundation Humanitarian Award recipient for his service to youth.

Stu lives in Southern California with his wife Candace (EduCare's co-founder) and enjoys spending time with their son in Oregon, meditating, biking, hiking in nature, puttering in the yard, being with family and friends, and following sports, especially the Los Angeles Dodgers.

Endnotes

1   Semigran, S. and Sindy Wilkinson. *Making the Best of Me: a Handbook for Student Excellence and Self-Esteem.* Educare Foundation. 1990, 2020.

2   Google English Dictionary, as provided by Oxford Languages.

3   Swensen, K., et al. "Parents' Use of Praise and Criticism in a Sample of Young Children Seeking Mental Health Services." J Pediatr Health Care. 2016 Jan-Feb. 30(1): 49-56. ncbi.nlm.nih.gov/pmc/articles/PMC4685017/.

4   Sparks, Dana. "Mayo Mindfulness: Overcoming Negative Self-Talk." May 29, 2019. newsnetwork.mayoclinic.org/discussion/mayo-mindfulness-overcoming-negative-self-talk/.

5   Dweck, Carol S. "The Perils and Promises of Praise." *Educational Leadership.* October 1, 2007. ascd.org/publications/educational-leadership/oct07/vol65/num02/The-Perils-and-Promises-of-Praise.aspx.

6   VenDeVelde, Christine. "Carol Dweck: Praising Intelligence: Costs to Children's Self-Esteem and Motivation. Stanford University Bing Times. November 1, 2007. bingschool.stanford.edu/news/carol-dweck-praising-intelligence-costs-childrens-self-esteem-and-motivation.

7   Anderson, Jenny. "The Stanford professor who pioneered praising kids for effort says we've totally missed

the point." *Quartz*. January 12, 2016. qz.com/587811/
stanford-professor-who-pioneered-praising-effort-sees-false-
praise-everywhere/.

8   Bennett, Collette. "Effective Praise in the Classroom."
ThoughtCo. January 21, 2020. thoughtco.com/effective-
praise-8161.

9   Dweck, Carol S. "The Perils and Promises of Praise."
Educational Leadership. October 1, 2007. ascd.org/
publications/educational-leadership/oct07/vol65/num02/
The-Perils-and-Promises-of-Praise.aspx.

10 Kornfield, Jack. *The Art of Forgiveness, Lovingkindness, and
Peace*. Bantam Publishing, 2008.

11 Fujawa, Judy. *Almost Everything You Need to Know about
Early Childhood Education*. Gryphon House. 1998. As quoted
on the Kaplan Early Learning Company webpage. kaplanco.
com/ii/opportunities-to-acknowledge-children.

12 Ramchandani, Jaya. "What Is Empathetic Listening?"
July 16, 2018. *We Learn We Grow*. blog.welearnwegrow.
community/what-is-empathic-listening-34a164f572a0.

13 Originally sourced from Covey, S. The Seven Habits of
Highly Effective People. Free Press. 2004.

14 Partnow, Susan. "The Five Practices of Compassionate
Listening." 2018. *The Compassionate Listening Project*. https://
sosspeace.org/wp-content/uploads/2018/04/The-Five-
Practices-of-Compassionate-ListeningSM-2.pdf.

15 Ramchandani, Jaya. "What Is Empathetic Listening?" July 16, 2018. *We Learn We Grow.* blog.welearnwegrow. community/what-is-empathic-listening-34a164f572a0.

16 Remen, Rachel Naomi. *Kitchen Table Wisdom: Stories that Heal.* Penguin Books. 2006.

17 Bogaczyk, Jeff. "The Power of Choice: Freedom Over Circumstances." August 23, 2017. *Mind For Life Blog.* mindforlife.org/power-of-choice-freedom-over-circumstances/.

18 Segal, Nick and Laura Segal. *On Your Terms.* Self-Published. 2018: 51.

19 Hulnick, Ron and Mary Hulnick. *Loyalty to Your Soul: The Heart of Spiritual Psychology.* Hay House. 2011.

20 Samuel, Mark and Sophie Chiche. *The Power of Personal Accountability.* Zephor Press. 2004: xvii.

21 Segal, Jeanne, Robinson, Lawrence, and Melinda Smith. "Conflict Resolution Skills." HelpGuide. October, 2020. helpguide.org/articles/relationships-communication/conflict-resolution-skills.htm.

22 Witchel, Alex. "At Lunch with Malachy McCourt: How a Rogue Turns Himself Into a Saint." July 29, 1998. *The New York Times.* nytimes.com/1998/07/29/books/lunch-with-malachy-mccourt-rogue-turns-himself-into-saint-blarney-fails-hide.html?pagewanted=all&src=pm.

23 Lawler, K., et al. "The Unique Effects of Forgiveness on Health: An Exploration of Pathways." J Behav Med. April 29, 2005. 157-67. pubmed.ncbi.nlm.nih.gov/15957571/.

24 McCullough, M., Pargament, K., and Carl Thoresen. *Forgiveness: Theory, Research, and Practice.* Guilford Press. 2001.

25 Geer, Beverly. June 3 2020. "Sometimes I just want it to stop. Talk of COVID, protests, looting, brutality. I lose my way." *Facebook.* facebook.com/beverly.geer.18/posts/10217030276296828.

26 Reinstein, Mara. "Michael J. Fox Talks Candidly About His Past, Present and Future, Saying 'I'm Still Lucky.'" November 20, 2020. *Parade Magazine.* parade.com/1122238/maramovies/michael-j-fox-says-he-is-lucky/.

27 Peralta, Daniel as quoted by Ryan, M.J. in *Attitudes of Gratitude: How to Give and Receive Joy Every Day of Your Life.* 1999. Conari Press.

28 Sprackling, Neil. "Making Good Use of a Crisis: Turning Challenges Into Opportunities." September 25, 2020. swissre.com/risk-knowledge/risk-perspectives-blog/turning-challenges-into-opportunities.html.

29 Langan-Reikhof, M., Avanni, A., and A. Janetti. "Sometimes the World Needs a Crisis: Turning Challenges Into Opportunities." April 10, 2017. brookings.edu/research/sometimes-the-world-needs-a-crisis-turning-challenges-into-opportunities/

30 Bridgenit. "Message from White Eagle, Hopi Indigenous on 03/16/2020." *Red Road Society.* April 1, 2020. redroadsociety.com/red-road-society/message-from-white-eagle-hopi-indigenous-on-03-16-2020.

31 DeGroot, Jacqueline. "Jewish Philanthropy: The Concept of Tzedakah." learningtogive.org/resources/jewish-philanthropy-concept-tzedakah.

32 Martinez, Mario as quoted by Northrup, Christiane in *Making Life Easy.* 2016. Hay House. Retrieved 9/28/21 from google.com/books/edition/Making_Life_Easy/hU76DwAAQBAJ?hl=en&gbpv=1&dq=D.

33 Marsh, Jason and Jill Suttie. "Five Ways Giving Is Good for You." *Greater Good Magazine.* December 13, 2010. greatergood.berkeley.edu/article/item/5_ways_giving_is_good_for_you.

34 Lyubomirsky, Sonja. *The How of Happiness.* Penguin Books. 2008.

35 McQuiston, Beth. "Why We Humans are Hard-Wired for Generosity." February 27, 2017. abbott.com/corpnewsroom/nutrition-health-and-wellness/giving-better-than-receiving.html.

36 McQuiston, Beth. "Why We Humans are Hard-Wired for Generosity."

Made in United States
Orlando, FL
13 November 2022